John and Sally McKenna's 'Bridgestone 100 Best' Guides give all the information you need to enjoy the best of Irish food. These restaurants are chosen for their cooking, their individuality, their creativity, and their value for money, each earning the right to call themselves one of the 100 Best.

The Bridgestone 100 Best Guides to Ireland are the most up-to-the-minute annual guides you can buy. Intensively and dedicatedly researched, with a wealth of detail and description of the chosen entries and written with humour and personal experience, these are the essential travelling companions. If you wish to find the very best of Ireland, you need to travel with John and Sally McKenna's Bridgestone Guides.

Readers' praise for the Bridgestone Guides:

'Informative, extremely well written and, above all, accurate ... I just wish there was something similar for England, Wales and Scotland'.
Mr. D.P., Thaxted, Essex.

'An excellent, entertaining and necessary guide to anyone hoping to find good food in this country'.
Mr. J. K., Crawley, Sussex.

'Your guidebook is a really good one because it does not mislead the reader but offers true and good advice. All the places we tried were all that your guide promised'.
Dr. C. B., Malta

'Without your knowledge and book we should not have had such a glorious holiday'.
Mrs. B. M., Athy, Co Kildare

GW00689559

First published in 1994 by
Estragon Press Ltd, Durrus, Bantry, Co Cork
© Estragon Press

Text copyright © John McKenna and Sally McKenna 1994
Illustrations copyright © Ken Buggy 1994
Maps copyright © Ken Buggy 1994
Cover photo © Lucy Johnston 1994

The moral right of the authors has been asserted

ISBN 1 874076 10 3

Printed by Colour Books Ltd, Baldoyle, Co Dublin Tel: (01) 832 5812
Designed by Karl Tsigdinos/Gold Star Media Ltd, Dublin Tel: (01) 260 0899
Typeset by Seton Music Graphics Ltd, Bantry, Co Cork Tel: (027) 50742
Cover Photo by Lucy Johnston, Garville Lane Studios Tel: (01) 496 0584

Whilst every effort has been made to ensure that the information
given in this book is accurate, the publishers and authors do not
accept responsibility for any errors or omissions.

Cover photo taken at Hunter's Hotel, *Rathnew, Co Wicklow.*

THE BRIDGESTONE
100 BEST RESTAURANTS
IN IRELAND 1994

JOHN MCKENNA

SALLY MCKENNA

With illustrations by Ken Buggy

ESTRAGON PRESS

For Paula Buckley

With thanks to:

Des Collins, Colm Conyngham, Karl, Lucy, Eddie, Elaine, Sarah Bates, Cynthia Harrison, Cathleen Buggy, Ray Buckley and John Harold, James O'Shea, Tom Owens, Robin Gourlay, Roger Lascelles, Ethna McKiernan, and Pat Ruane

JOES

John McKenna was born in Belfast and educated both there and in Dublin, where he practised as a barrister before turning to writing in 1989. His work appears in newspapers and magazines in Ireland and the U.K. In 1993 he won the Glenfiddich Regional Writer of the Year Award for journalism.

Sally McKenna was born in Kenya, and brought up on the Pacific island of Fiji before coming to Ireland in 1982. She cooked professionally before turning to writing about food and restaurants. She is a member of the accreditation panel of the Bio-dynamic Agricultural Association in Ireland.

Ken Buggy was born in Dublin in 1947 and has spent most of his working life abroad. He now lives in Kinsale with his wife Cathleen and their four children.

JOHN McKENNA and SALLY McKENNA won the first André Simon Special Commendation Award in 1992 for the second edition of The Bridgestone Irish Food Guide.

Contents

*B*RIDGESTONE

BRIDGESTONE IS JAPAN'S LARGEST tyre manufacturer and one of the top three in the world. Founded in 1931, the company has striven to maintain an emphasis on technological advancement and service while expanding the scale and scope of its operations. As a result the company is recognised as a leader in tyre manufacturing and technology.

Bridgestone tyres are presently sold in more than 150 countries. There are twelve manufacturing plants in Japan with others throughout the world including the U.S.A. and Australia. Bridgestone now also manufactures its tyres in Europe following the acquisition in 1988 of the Firestone Tyre and Rubber Company.

They manufacture tyres for many different vehicles, from trucks and buses to passenger cars and motor-cycles. Its commercial vehicle tyres enjoy a worldwide reputation for superior cost-per-kilometre performance, and its aircraft tyres are used by more than 100 international airlines. Many Japanese cars imported to Ireland arrive with Bridgestone tyres and a host of exotic sports cars including Ferrari, Lamborghini, Porsche, Jaguar and TVR are now fitted with Bridgestone tyres as original equipment.

Bridgestone is at the forefront of tyre research and development. Its proving ground in Kuroiso City, Japan covers 400,000 square metres and consists of a 3.5 kilometre banked test track and skid pan which together contain more than 40 different road surfaces. Bridgestone also operate an advanced R&D facility in Kodaira, Japan. Testing focuses on a wide range of features including directional stability, skid resistance, durability, abrasion resistance, riding comfort and noise reduction. All this data is then put to valuable use in the development of new and better tyres. Bridgestone is now the most technologically advanced tyre manufacturer in the world.

In June 1990 Bridgestone (Ireland) Ltd was established as a subsidiary of the multinational Bridgestone Corporation to take over the distribution of its tyres in Ireland. The company operates from its offices and warehouse in Tallaght in Dublin where it stocks a wide range of passenger car, commercial vehicle and earthmover tyres. Bridgestone staff also provide sales, technical and delivery services all over the country.

● *Bridgestone tyres are available from tyre dealers throughout Ireland. For further information contact Bridgestone (Ireland) Ltd., Unit A30, Greenhills Industrial Estate, Tallaght, Dublin 24. Tel: (01) 452 7766 Fax: (01) 452 7478*

How To Use This Book

THIS BOOK IS arranged alphabetically, firstly by virtue of County names — County Cavan is followed by County Clare which is followed by County Cork, and so on — and then within the counties the individual entries are arranged alphabetically — so Longueville House, in north Cork, will follow after Lettercollum House, which is in south west Cork. Entries in Northern Ireland are included in a separate section. The maps in the book are intended only as a general guide and we recommend that they be used in conjunction with an accurate Ordnance Survey map.

All visits to the restaurants, hotels, cafés and eateries included in this book were made anonymously. All meals were paid for and any offers of discounts or gifts were refused.

In cases where we felt the food served in a restaurant was of such a special, unique, stature, where the best Irish ingredients were presented in their finest possible state, we have marked the entry with a ★.

In cases where we felt the food served in a restaurant was of special interest we have marked the entry with a ➡, meaning that the entry is worthy of making a detour in order to enjoy the food.

In cases where we feel a restaurant offers excellent value for money, we have marked these entries with a £.

Whilst opening times are given for restaurants, it is always advisable to telephone in advance and check opening times when booking a meal. Note also that many restaurants in the south and the west of the country are seasonal, closing during the winter months, whilst others alter their opening hours out of season.

Prices: the prices quoted represent an average price for a meal for one person, without wine. Where a restaurant offers meals at a set price, this is the price we have quoted and, should you choose from the à la carte, you should expect to pay more.

All prices and details are correct at the time of going to press but, given the volatile nature of restaurants and the peripatetic nature of restaurant staff, we are unable to accept any responsibility should the circumstances of any of the entries change.

Finally, we greatly appreciate receiving reports, suggestions and criticisms from readers.

The Bridgestone Awards

STARRED RESTAURANTS ★

Ballymaloe House, Shanagarry, Co Cork
Clifford's, Cork City, Co Cork
Drimcong House, Moycullen, Co Galway
Dunworley Cottage, Butlerstown, Co Cork
Longueville House, Mallow, Co Cork
Roscoff, Belfast, Co Antrim
Truffles, Sligo, Co Sligo

RESTAURANTS WORTH A DETOUR ➡

Assolas House, Kanturk, Co Cork
Beech Hill Country Hotel, Derry, Co Londonderry
Destry Rides Again, Clifden, Co Galway
Erriseask House, Ballyconneely, Co Galway
Eugene's Restaurant, Ballyedmond, Co Wexford
Heir Island Restaurant, Heir Island, Co Cork
Ivory Tower Restaurant, Cork, Co Cork
Lacken House, Kilkenny, Co Kilkenny
Lettercollum House, Timoleague, Co Cork
Nick's Warehouse, Belfast, Co Antrim
Oystercatcher Restaurant, Oysterhaven, Co Cork
Packies, Kenmare, Co Kerry
Shiro Japanese Dinner House, Ahakista, Co Cork
Strawberry Tree, Killarney, Co Kerry

RESTAURANTS WHICH OFFER
EXCELLENT VALUE FOR MONEY £

Destry Rides Again, Clifden, Co Galway
Drimcong House, Moycullen, Co Galway
Eugene's Restaurant, Ballyedmond, Co Wexford
Lettercollum House, Timoleague, Co Cork
Mainistir House, Kilronan, Aran Island, Co Galway
Packie's, Kenmare, Co Kerry
Roscoff, Belfast, Co Antrim

Introduction

IT IS TRADITIONAL, amongst annual guides, to begin the book with a prefatory gripe.

Tradition has it that there should be some niggling feature, which has slowly become either a fashionable niggling feature or a regrettably recurring niggling feature, which the authors or editors must — simply must — get off their respective chests.

It may be the insistence that dogs are only permitted into dining rooms if they are non-smokers, for example, which has enraged the authors during the course of the year. Perhaps it will be the prevalence of pony tails amongst male staff. The playing of certain types of music may suddenly seem to have become de rigeur, much to the dislike of the patient inspectors as they set about the business of disseminating a meal. So, whilst 'Kind Of Blue' by Miles Davis may accord with certain sensibilities, those same sensibilities may be outraged by the bleating of Elton John, or the boredom of Eric Clapton, or the waywardness of Leonard Bernstein conducting Edward Elgar. Thus, this year, the tirade may be against the hapless Mr John, or the scarcely-lamented Bernstein.

Or it may be the truly disconcerting habit amongst youthful staff of saying 'Have a good one!' (a good what? Coronary? Fall from a cliff-top?) which proves to be the niggling feature of the previous 12 months. Likewise, it may be a certain food fashion which has one grinding teeth and muttering under-breath oaths. The prevalence of mangetout; spaghetti with mushrooms in a cream sauce or the endless misspelling of 'tagliatelle'; the umpteenth dish with sun-dried tomatoes; commercial ice creams being fobbed off as 'Our own homemade ices'. Any one thing is usually fit to be fried by an enraged author just before the guide goes off to press.

We have traditionally steered clear of this stratagem, feeling always that it was merely a mechanism to secure newspaper publicity when the book appeared — 'Guide authors urge stiff sentences for staff who refer to Puligny-Montrachet as "a cheeky little wine you're just certain to love"'. It has always seemed to us more important to celebrate the good rather than annoint the bad with greater attention.

The Bridgestone 100 Best Guides are only ever about the best food we can find — a hundred restaurants represents the merest fraction of those in Ireland who open their doors for business, so having found them we tend to feel that they are worthy of our acclamation, though we hope we do point to any shortfalls which may afflict the places we choose. We are more concerned to uncover the creative and the correct. But, having said that, there is one feature of modern restaurant cooking which has proved to be popular, and proved to be a cause for regret. We mean the kidney plate.

Kidney plates do not hold kidneys, of course. In real life, kidney plates should be confined to their valuable work in hospitals — 'Nurse, pass the forceps and hold the kidney plate for me please' — where they are essential, useful and their function is to be welcomed.

Where they do not belong is in restaurants. The mere sight of their arrival — the kitchen doors swing back and the waitress comes out with one dish in each tea-towel wrapped hand — has now led to a little game which we play with each other: 'I bet this is two florets of broccoli, one floret of cauliflower, six mange tout and a thimble of potato gratin'.

'I say it's going to be some batons of carrot, a plain boiled potato and a handful of fried cabbage with shards of bacon and a little cream'. We then wager a few bob on the outcome.

In this way, when the dreaded kidney plates are placed on the table by the waitress (who always says 'Plates are very hot, be careful'. Of course they are: they have just been lifted out of a microwave oven) we hope to make light of this culinary miasma, this regrettable but prevalent occurrence.

It is regrettable for this simple reason. One of us will have chosen fish from the à la carte, and one will be having a daube of beef from the table d'hôte. Yet the vegetables, this bland array chosen as much for their colour contrast as anything else, are offered as being suitable for both dishes. Patently they are not. Patently it would not have been very difficult to devise a selection of vegetables which would complement the separate dishes. Patently the kitchen has not bothered to do this.

It is the laziness of this action which offends most, as much as the disregard for the dish of vegetables themselves, the feeling that they are mere filler, stodge for bulking out the centrepiece which will sit on the main plate to the right of the kidney plate. The action is a hangover from the days when all that mattered in an Irish meal was that there be a plenitude of protein on the plate in the shape of a hank of beef or a hank of pork or a breast of chicken. We have come a long way from those days. But the vegetable plate, that relic of the dark ages of Irish cooking, remains, casting its kidney-shaped shadow.

In the whirlwind of creativity and culinary invention which has swept through the doors of Irish restaurants in the last decade and which is one factor which unifies those places chosen in this book, the kidney plate is the only careless blemish. It is so easily correctible as to make its presence even more infuriating.

So we would like to see something done about this blemish, and we promise to applaud those who, in future, act to improve the lowly status of vegetables which is implicit in the kidney plate, those who work to raise the blessed things to the stature of forming their own course — which is where a good creamy potato gratin belongs, after all — and we think most people will be happier as a result. It won't quite be the equivalent of world peace, but let's be thankful for the small things.

JOHN MCKENNA, SALLY MCKENNA
Durrus, County Cork.

MACNEAN BISTRO

Blacklion, Co Cavan Tel: (072) 53022
Vera and Nevan Maguire

A curious sense of culinary schizophrenia enlivens the MacNean Bistro. Set in a small front room on the main street in Blacklion, the cooking is shared by Vera and Nevan, mother and son. There are two menus, an à la carte and the 'chef's special', and they're as different as chalk and cheese. Gastronomes must opt for the chef's special, the responsibility of son Nevan, a cook who 'goes to bed with cookery books' says Mr Maguire Snr. His food is inspired by those whom he has read, and enlivened by a skill which, in parts, verges on the virtuosi.

Partridge, pigeon, quail and fowl dominate the menu, with fish correctly restricted to what could be bought fresh. Occasionally dishes get dandied up in name only — a salmon 'tartlette' looks and tastes much like a quiche, 'roast sirloin with potato gratin' is no more than a steak — but presentation in every case is exceptionally attractive and dishes such as pan fried lamb with black pudding mousse, where eyes of lamb fillet are sealed with the mousse and served with pickles and minuscule vegetables, are clever and distinctive and show the direction of a young chef just poised to conquer — if only his clientele would let him have his head, for many of the Northern customers who cross the border to Blacklion are stoically conservative.

But it is in the desserts (and again — always always opt for the 'chef's special' desserts rather than those in the glass cabinet which so dominates the room) that Nevan Maguire's skills are best exemplified. A chocolate plate collection of white, milk and dark chocolate confections is exquisitely beautiful and rich in chocolate, just as it describes itself. A restrained baked pear is unleashed into pure extravagance by its sticky caramel sauce, nougat ice cream wears a Philip Tracey hat of spun sugar. You leave the restaurant on a high, with the narcotic command of these desserts still coursing through your veins.

Open 12.30pm-3pm, 6pm-9.30pm Tue-Sun
Closed Xmas and Good Fri
Average Price: lunch £9.50, dinner £16.50
Credit Cards: Visa, Access/Master, Amex
No Service Charge
Wine Licence
No Wheelchair Access
Children — welcome
Vegetarian food available with prior notice
On the main street in Blacklion.

CLAIRE'S RESTAURANT

Ballyvaughan, Co Clare Tel: (065) 77029
Claire Walsh

In Claire's Restaurant, in the snaky little water's edge village of Ballyvaughan, at the foot of the brooding hills of the Burren, you will, on a good night, see more people completely and enjoyably at their ease than at anytime and in any other place which you can likely remember. This is the sort of restaurant that summons relaxed, boozy laughter, whether you happen to be feeling in that vibrant holiday mood or not, whether the place is packed with duos and quartets or troops of bikers and hikers or flora and fauna explorers, and whether it is Saturday night in August or Wednesday in May.

Everyone is here to eat the local foods — mussels feuillete, baked Burren cheese, fresh lobster cooked to toothy perfection, sweet Burren lamb which melts in the mouth — and to allow the glam young women who deal with everything so pertly and persuasively to look after you, and everyone is here to get on with the business of raising the roof. Leaving, maybe sometime in the wee small hours, you will find yourself promising yourself that you will return here soon, soonest. For, when you are in Clare, you really want to be in Claire's.

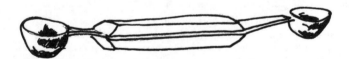

Open 7pm-10pm Mon-Sat during Jul & Aug, Mon-Fri during May, Jun & Sept
Closed Oct-Xmas (then 1 week open), New Year-Easter (open some weekends during this latter period).
Average Price: dinner £15-£20
10% Service Charge
Credit Cards: Visa, Access
Wine Licence
Wheelchair Access
Children — welcome
Vegetarian dish always on menu
In the centre of Ballyvaughan.

BARRTRA SEAFOOD RESTAURANT

Lahinch, Co Clare Tel: (065) 81280
Paul & Theresa O'Brien

Looking from the window in his little restaurant which overlooks Liscannor Bay, Paul O'Brien counts in the returning little red fishing boats and, if he sees them going out and then sees them coming in, he knows that the speciality of the Barrtrá — fresh lobster — will be on the menu tonight. Oysters, home-smoked salmon, smudgy home-made rolls and Kilshanny cheeses make up the rest of this simple, just-right menu, a perfect holiday-time place with the intelligence to play to its strengths and to keep things simple and satisfying.

Open 1pm-3pm, 6pm-9pm Mon-Sat, 1pm-3pm Sun
Closed late Oct-end March (Xmas and New Year parties by arrangement)
Average Price: dinner £16, Sun lunch £8, weekday lunch £2-£10
Credit Cards: Visa, Access
No Service Charge
Wine Licence
No Wheelchair Access
Children — welcome early evenings
Private functions possible (seating 28)
Recommended for Vegetarians
Signposted from the Lahinch-Milltown Malbay Road.

MAC CLOSKEY'S

Bunratty House Mews, Bunratty, Co Clare Tel: (061) 364082
Gerry & Marie Mac Closkey

The Mac Closkey banquets, given every night in this restored basement restaurant, are the antithesis to those ladled out in nearby castles and keeps, where tourists may find themselves enshrined for a night in medieval Ireland.

Gerry Mac Closkey's cooking is true and creative, and where other banquets are clichéd, Mac Closkey's five-course specials are contemporary and individual. Instead, the food here is calm and very polished, and Mr Mac Closkey's work with the great staples of the area such as Burren lamb, west coast mussels, and other local ingredients locate the true flavours of these fine foods with unerring accuracy. And, should you tire of finger lickin', in Mac Closkey's you will find more cutlery and crockery in use than almost any other restaurant.

Open 7pm-10pm Tue-Sat
Closed Xmas-end Jan
Average Price: dinner £26
Credit Cards: Visa, Access/Master, Amex, Diners
10% Service Charge
Full Licence
No Wheelchair Access
Children — no facilities
Vegetarian menu available with prior notice
Take the N18 from Limerick and the restaurant is signposted in Bunratty.

SHEEDY'S SPA VIEW HOTEL

Lisdoonvarna, Co Clare Tel: (065) 74026 Fax: 74555
Frank & Patsy Sheedy

Sheedy's may look like just another paid-up member of that multitude of mature but unprepossessing hotels found the length and breadth of Ireland. Walk inside and the décor is unsurprisingly unsurprising, and you may even see those fabulous old ladies you half expected to find in a fading spa town like Lisdoonvarna, sitting just where you expected to find them, complete with Alan Bennett dialogue.
'That's lovely that, isn't it', one old darling says to her lady companion. The companion replies with silence.
'What is it?', asks the first.
But Sheedy's is different. Frankie Sheedy cooks proper food, real food, not the sort of food you expect to find in an hotel in a drowsy spa town: local black pudding with stewed apple and sweet onions; gravadlax served with nasturtiums, borage flowers, salad leaves, baby tomatoes and cashew nuts; breast of chicken amidst a pool of toothy, creamy yellow lentils; Irish blue shark on a bed of crisp kale underlaid with ribbons of carrot.

Open 6.30pm-9pm Mon-Sun
Closed mid-Mar-end Sept
Average Price: dinner £18-£25
Credit Cards: Visa, Access/Master, Amex, Diners
No Fixed Service Charge
Full Pub Licence
Wheelchair Access (to restaurant and gents toilet)
Children — welcome
Vegetarian dishes always offered
Lisdoonvarna town centre.

ADÈLES

Main Street, Schull, Co Cork Tel: (028) 28459
Adèle Connor

Adèle Connor's bakery, coffee shop and lunchtime eating house
has been one of the most essential fixtures of Schull for more than
a decade, now, a place always characterised by an exactitude which
meant that things, no matter how small, no matter how trivial, were
always done right.

The shop and restaurant have a gentle, light-hearted soul, the youthful
energy of bare boards and simple seats, the satisfaction which comes
from finding yourself in here and knowing you are in exactly the right
place, knowing that this is where you want to be.

As if this was not enough, Simon Connor opened up Adèles during
the evenings in the season of 1993, with a simple menu that revelled
in clean, vibrant tasting starters, taste-suffused pasta dishes, syrupy
desserts, and added a splendid new dimension to this splendid place.

Mr Connor will roast red and yellow peppers and pair them with some
feta cheese and a light dressing for a famishsome starter, or plate some
cold meats, sourced from here and there in Counties Cork and Kerry,
or have you drooling over a superb chunky pork terrine served with a
beetroot jelly. His pasta dishes can include a truly fine spaghetti with
parsley pesto, or angel hair pasta with mussels in a spicy tomato sauce,
or pappardelle with chicken liver and marjoram. Happily, he manages
never to concede a complexity of flavours in his pasta cooking: the food
looks simple, but the tastes are involved, and thereby involving.

The teaming of everything, from pasta to sauce, from dressing to
dish, right down to the crockery and the wines on offer, is splendidly
appropriate, and the generous prices mean that another bottle of wine
may well be discovered which has your name on it. No matter. Just let
the spirit of youth you find here infuse itself into your evening and
your being.

Open 9.30am-10.30pm Mon-Sun (check out of season)
Closed Nov-Apr (open three weeks at Xmas)
Average Price: dinner £8-£15
No Credit Cards
10% Service Charge for parties of six or more
Wine Licence
Wheelchair Access, but not to toilets
Children — high chairs and half portions
Vegetarian options always available
At the top of the hill in the town centre.

AHERNE'S SEAFOOD BAR

163 North Main Street, Youghal, Co Cork Tel: (024) 92424 Fax: 93633
The Fitzgibbon family

There is a happy sense of timelessness about Aherne's. It may be
engendered by the fact that it is currently the third generation of
Fitzgibbons who run this handsome place, but it may equally be the
true sense of professionalism and seriousness of purpose which the
family espouse and practice which makes the place ever-enduring.
This seriousness of purpose manifests itself as a determination to get
things done properly, whether that is with the simple food cooked in
the bar — seafood chowder, some native oysters, smoked salmon pâté,
a crab and prawn salad — or in the cloistering enfolds of the dining
room, when David Fitzgibbon's fish cookery is given free and full
rein — pan-fried scallops, monkfish and prawns in a coral sauce,
monkfish with Pernod and fennel, brill and prawns in Chablis. This
is very classic fish cooking, with the classic accompaniments ever on
hand and a near-certain rate of success. Indeed, a success in Aherne's
may gift you with some of the finest fish cooking it is possible to enjoy,
and you will go away and find that you have become a Cod Bore, or a
Brill Bore, anxious to tell all and sundry about that fabulous fillet, that
soulful shellfish . . .

Open 12.30pm-2pm, 6.30pm-9.30pm Mon-Sun (bar meals 11am-10pm Mon-Sun)
Closed Xmas week
Average Price: lunch £13.50, dinner £21, (bar meals from £5)
Credit Cards: Visa, Access/Master
10% Service Charge
Full Pub Licence
Wheelchair Access (incl disabled toilet)
Children — welcome
Vegetarian dishes available with notice
Centre of Youghal town.

ANNIE'S
Main Street , Ballydehob, Co Cork Tel: (028) 37292
Dano and Annie Barry

Annie Barry has the bestest, nicest, manner of any restaurant owner
in the country. Her pacific nature with kids is legendary — Mrs Barry
herself, of course, is too modest to agree with this — but she works her
spell on adult kids with the same surreptitious ease, and quickly has
you boggle-eyed and goo-goo with anticipation for the treat that is
dinner in Annie's.

The restaurant is just a single room with tables in multiples of pairs,
nice and bright in summertime if you choose an early evening dinner,
with drinks across the road in Levis's pub while you choose from the
menu. Mr Barry doesn't try to do too much — and doesn't need to do
too much — to coax the very best from his good ingredients. The most
preparation a piece of Sally Barnes's super smoked salmon ever needs
is a squidge of lemon; with scallops as big and fat and coral-clawed as
the ones you find in here, then a cream and white wine sauce may
almost seem superfluous, but the sauce will be generous and precise,
as generous and precise as an apricot sauce around a piece of finely
roasted duck. The cooking may be light in execution, but it is deep
in savour.

Right down to the very simple things — some luscious boiled spuds
which you gobble up with the appetite of someone who has been hacking
turf all day long, some baked cod or maybe, the regular's choice, a super-
duper steak and some fab chips — Annie's gets it right. The temperament
of this little place never changes, and never needs to, for who would
tamper with a classic.

Open 12.30pm-2.30pm, 6.30pm-9.30pm Tue-Sat (dinner only off season)
Closed Xmas, Oct and bank holidays
Average Price: lunch £6.50, dinner £20
Credit Cards: Visa, Access/Master
No Service Charge
Wine Licence
Wheelchair Access to restaurant but not to toilets
Children — welcome, but no facilities
Recommended for Vegetarians, with notice
In the centre of Ballydehob.

ARBUTUS LODGE

Montenotte, Cork city, Co Cork Tel: (021) 501237 Fax: 502893
Michael & Declan Ryan

Recent years have seen a greater informality make its way into the serving of food in Arbutus and, nowadays, one of the biggest attractions of the hotel is the very modern and delicious dishes served in the bar at lunchtime. Whilst relatively simple food, it always reveals the Ryan family's continuing interest in food fashions and trends and is always executed with a professionalism that is the hallmark of this handsome and enduring operation.

Whilst the bar food is just as suitable as the more formal cooking of the dining room when it comes to matching a good bottle of wine from the extraordinary wine list to accompany it, one may want to wander into the more complex dishes which Helen Ward prepares in the restaurant to truly do justice to this most magisterial list, one of the very finest to be found in Ireland. The list continues to attract plaudits and awards every year, and it deserves each and every one of them.

Open 1pm-2pm, 7pm-9.30pm Mon-Sat
Closed Xmas
Average Price: lunch £12.50, dinner £21
Credit Cards: Visa, Access/Master, Amex, Diners
No Service Charge
Full Licence
Wheelchair Access
Children — high chairs and half portions
Vegetarian dishes always available
Cork city centre, signposted from the Cork-Dublin road.

ASSOLAS COUNTRY HOUSE ➡

Kanturk, Co Cork Tel: (029) 50015 Fax: (029) 50795
Joe and Hazel Bourke

Hazel Bourke's cooking would be impressive wherever you happily
happened to chance upon it, but it must be said that her feminine and
instinctively correct approach to food seems unusually apposite when
you happily happen upon it in the feminine and instinctively correct
ambience of Assolas.

This is one of the nicest country houses, not at all showy or blowy, but
someplace quiet, genteel. Mrs Bourke's cooking is an echo of the house:
charming, unpretentious, striking a fine balance between the necessary
formality which the house insists upon, and yet gifting the theatre of
dinner with a girlish spontaneity and creativity that suffuses the food.

It is perhaps her feel for freshness in food and in garden herbs which is
her principal signature — before dinner, Mrs Bourke will be out in the
garden at Assolas, gathering, collecting, selecting — but there is also a
terrific devotion to taste — simple, pure, natural, tastes extracted from
each ingredient — which shows a cook who has never lost sight of
what she wants to achieve: mussels from Kenmare may be bundled up
in a pastry case, or the shellfish may be prawns and scallops from
Union Hall, or you may be succoured instead by the saline grace of
Roscarbery oysters.

Neither culinary pyrotechnics nor arrogant ego is allowed any rein in the
kitchen, so breast of duck will be accompanied by glazed apples, loin of
lamb will have a rosemary jus and a mint jelly, and you enjoy food which
is recognisably itself and, best of all, has scents and flavours and savours
which are implicit, understood, etched deep in our culinary memories
from times past.

Joe and Hazel Bourke are the second generation of the family to run
Assolas, and their solicitousness and charm has seen this fine house
begin to acquire the reputation it deserves for food, for service, for
offering the essence of creativity and hospitality.

Open 7pm-8.30pm Mon-Sun (non-residents booking essential)
Closed Nov-mid March
Average Price: dinner £27
Credit Cards: Visa, Access/Master, Amex, Diners
No Service Charge (tipping not expected)
Full Licence
Wheelchair Access to restaurant but not toilets
Children — no facilities
Vegetarian options available on request
On the Mallow to Killarney road, follow signs to Kanturk. Four-and-a-half miles before
Kanturk you will see signs for Assolas House.

BALLYMALOE HOUSE ★

Shanagarry, Midleton, Co Cork Tel: (021) 652531 Fax: 652021
Ivan and Myrtle Allen

Myrtle Allen's philosophy of food is durable, homespun, simple. First, encourage a circle of producers around you to produce the best foods they can and support them as best you can. Keep everything local and thereby enjoy the benefit of foods which express themselves in terms of the micro-climate in which they are produced and reared. Attempt to be as self-sufficient as you can: grow your own spuds, make your own chutneys, produce as much of the food you need through your own endeavours.

When it comes to the cooking of this food, do it from scratch and do it with ingredients as pristinely fresh as possible. No egotism must blunt the edge of the cooking: just allow the food to speak of and for itself. Then, when it comes to serving the food, do it simply, but courteously and as graciously as you can. Deep-coloured dining rooms, good paintings to lift the soul, good wines to salve the spirit, all done with the maximum dialogue between customer and cook, a culinary conversation.

This is a simple modus, and Myrtle Allen has never lost sight of this creed of simplicity, this respect for plainness in thinking and cooking, in twenty five years. During that time, the philosophy of Ballymaloe has remained consistent: respect for the fruits of the land, air and sea. Respect for the long-held culinary codes which best transform these fruits. Respect for the person who will enjoy the fruits of the cook's labours and, just as important, respect demanded for the efforts of the cook and respect for the culinary arts.

Many people find it difficult to see this simplicity at work. But there are many, still, who see in the Ballymaloe philosophy a logical, conscientious, concerned and kind way of working with the world. For them it is this deep thread, just as much as the delicious presentations on a plate, which makes Ballymaloe special.

Open 12.30pm-1.30pm, 7pm-10pm Mon-Sun
Closed Xmas
Average Price: lunch from £10, dinner £30
Credit Cards: Visa, Access/Master, Amex, Diners
No Service Charge
Full Licence
Wheelchair Access to restaurant but not easily to toilets
Children — high chairs, half portions for under 9yrs
Recommended for Vegetarians
Ballymaloe House is signposted from the N25.

BILLY MACKESY'S BAWNLEIGH HOUSE

Ballinhassig, Co Cork Tel: (021) 771333
Billy Mackesy

There is a lot of Billy Mackesy's personality tied up and inextricably expressed in his food. He is a large, thoughtful man who can sometimes seem quietly quiet, though you find yourself always on the alert for an explosion of volubility. His cooking, meantime, is generous in flavour and in portion, as welcoming as it is challenging, and the surprises of sharp personality that peek through its subtleties are refreshing: like Mackesy himself, there is a lot of consideration under the surface.
He likes to use robust cuts of meat and game: pink pigeon breasts, breaded sweetbreads topped with citrus fruit, a venison steak that has been first marinated and then char-grilled. But he is fluent also with fish, such as a dish where salmon is first smoked and then, in an inspired move, is served simply with potato, or where brill is teamed with the serenest of all herbs, basil, in a cream sauce. But there is never a loss of delicacy in the cooking, and volume does not compensate for flavour.
The service is memorable in its humour, enthusiasm and knowledge, and you feel the restaurant is run as a team, by a team. The interior design, arriving somewhere close to a typical Irish front room without the religious portraits or the television sets, is ruggedly unfashionable. But, because everything is done right and done so spiritedly, you find yourself pleased by this lack of artifice, and it makes Mackesy's a place where you can relax and let your hair down.

Open 7.30pm-10.30pm Tue-Sat, from 12.30pm Sun
Closed Xmas
Average Price: lunch £12, dinner £18
Credit Cards: Visa, Access/Master, Diners
No Service Charge
Full Pub Licence
Wheelchair Access
Children — welcome with prior notice
Vegetarian meals with prior notice
From the bridge at Half-Way village take the road to Kinsale. The restaurant is on the right after about 3 miles.

LA BIGOUDENNE

28 McCurtain Street, Fermoy, Co Cork Tel: (025) 32832
Rodolphe and Noelle Semeria

La Bigoudenne restaurant is as prototypically French as the
ceremonial, luridly-phallic pointed hat which gives the restaurant its
name. During the day it is a simple café with wonderful food to restore
the traveller: filled baguettes, chunky pâtés, home-made soups, but the
speciality of the restaurant, and one that makes it worth travelling any
distance to try, are the crêpes: savoury ones — filled with ham and egg,
egg and cheese, chicken and mushroom with cream, salad and blue
cheese; and sweet ones — filled with stewed apple, chocolate, pear and
ice-cream. They are splendid on-the-road food, giving energy,
brightening the soul.

At night, napery comes out and everything is more formal: a glass of
kir to begin, then veal with some ceps, or fresh river trout, or sweet
fresh lobster with butter. The food, the techniques and the styling
come straight from the French provinces and allow for simple direct
tastes and a confident, calm atmosphere. In this neck of the woods,
La Bigoudenne is vital.

Open 12.15pm-5.30pm, 7.15pm-10pm Tue-Sat
Open all year incl Xmas
Average Price: lunch £3.50-£4.50, dinner £14.25
Credit Cards: Visa, Access/Master
No Service Charge
Wine Licence
Wheelchair Access
Children — welcome, no special facilities
Vegetarian options available on the day-time menu
Fermoy town centre.

BLAIR'S COVE RESTAURANT

Durrus, Co Cork Tel: (027) 61127
Philippe & Sabine De Mey

Philippe De Mey runs a calmly orchestrated dining theatre in the
beautiful big old barn that is Blair's Cove. The room has a flavour
of medieval ages and perhaps the best way to get the best out of an
evening in the Cove is to choose something from amongst the grilled
meats which they produce on the wood-fired grill which flickers and
flames away at the head of the dining room, much as if we were back
in the days of sack and Falstaff. The natural fire and the alluring odour
of wood smoke which the grill gives to racks of lamb and hanks of beef
is irresistible.

Ally this with a hungry raid on the great monument of an hors d'oeuvre
table for a selection of pâtés, some smoked and marinated fish, maybe
a clean soupçon of pickled vegetables, then follow with ripe local
cheeses from Durrus or Gubbeen with crisp cumin biscuits, finish with
some well-made chocolate mousse, and it is all too easy to build a fine
meal. In the vaguely gothic ambience, the vaguely gothic roasts, grills,
pickles and puddings are just right.

Open 7.30pm-9.30pm Tue-Sat (open Mon, Jul and Aug)
Closed Nov-mid Mar
Average Price: dinner £23
Credit Cards: Visa, Access/Master, Amex, Diners
10% Service Charge
Restaurant Licence
Wheelchair Access to restaurant but not to toilets
Children — high chairs and half portions
One Vegetarian main course served each evening
One-and-a-half miles from Durrus on the Durrus-Goleen/Barleycove road.

CHEZ YOUEN

Baltimore, Co Cork Tel: (028) 20136
Youen Jacob

It is the sauces which give away Youen Jacob's easy affinity with
his craft. An emulsion of mayonnaise in which to dunk your shellfish
platter. A hollandaise of angelic lightness under a fillet of salmon.
Cream with green peppercorns for roasted beef. With each dish, the
sauce is as essential as the principal ingredient, indeed, with fish and
shellfish, it can seem that the sauce is truly the star, the real performer
on a stage set by the fish. It is simple food, perfectly done, and at
lunchtime the fish and shellfish and sauces marry so well with a bottle
of Muscadet that you might just forget that there is any work to be
done. When you get around to eating some tarte tatin, the best tarte
tatin in your life, you wish the crumbly, intensity could last forever.
The music is always good, the atmosphere unpretentiousness, and
there is fun to be had.

Open 12.30pm-3pm, 6.30pm-11pm
Closed Nov-Mar (open for a period around Xmas). No lunches Sept-Easter
Average Price: lunch £12.50-£28, dinner £19.50-£32
Credit Cards: Visa, Access/Master, Amex, Diners
No Service Charge
Wine Licence
Wheelchair Access (1 step to restaurant, no access to toilet)
Children — welcome
Vegetarian dishes available on request
In centre of Baltimore, overlooking the bay.

CLIFFORD'S ★

18 Dyke Parade, Cork, Co Cork Tel: (021) 275333
Michael and Deirdre Clifford

As the only volunteer boy in a domestic science class, Michael Clifford remembers, 'I scoffed the semolina and even the tapioca, but my favourite treat then was toast cut thick and spread with good beef dripping. The jellied meat juices seeped through into the soft centre and liquified pleasantly against the tongue: to this day I am ready to put in a good word for my favourite'.

In his professional life, however, Mr Clifford has put in good deeds, rather than just good words, for his favourite foods. His cooking strikes an original and entirely appropriate balance between competing disciplines: sumptuous and comforting, yet based on relatively simple ingredients; cosmopolitan, yet happiest when working with something grown as close to the restaurant as possible. His food is modern in style and technique, but he can manage to evoke a taste that seems age-old and yet — and this is vital — he avoids any sense of that dread nostalgia which so restricts Irish cuisine.

No one else can make a velouté of chicken with lentils and pearl barley which is so staggeringly warming that you feel you could wager the health of nations on it. No one else can make a simple dish of smoked haddock into a warm salad so suffused with smoky, tensile loveliness. His improvisation on Edward Twomey's Clonakilty Black Pudding feeds the mealy heat of the pudding with tender little blinis and a purée of local mushrooms and the result is a dish which works because of well-understood understatement.

Indeed, all of Mr Clifford's cooking, it seems, returns to that boyhood memory: warm, tactile, coaxing tastes which melt and liquify, which sustain and delight. This romance with the whole business of running a restaurant makes Clifford's one of the most enjoyable places to eat in Ireland, for his staff are hopelessly happy in their work and Michael's wife Deirdre augments the chef's shyness with her bubbly confidence.

Open 12.30pm-2.30pm Tue-Fri, 7pm-10.30pm Mon-Sat
Closed Xmas Day and bank holidays
Average Price: lunch £12.50, dinner £28
Credit Cards: Visa, Access/Master, Amex, Diners
No Service Charge
Restaurant Licence
No Wheelchair Access
Children — welcome, but no facilities
Special Vegetarian menu composed with prior discussion, £19
Clifford's is a minute's walk from Jury's hotel: turn left, then right and at the first set of traffic lights you will see the restaurant on the corner.

LA COQUILLE

Main Street, Schull, Co Cork Tel: (028) 28642
Jean-Michel Cahier

Both menu and wine list in Jean-Michel Cahier's restaurant are stubbornly mute and uninformative in that somewhat arrogant French way of doing things. Scallops with garlic butter. Smoked salmon. Monkfish with green and red peppers. Rack of lamb. Fillet of steak. Tarte tatin. Ice-cream.

This lack of elaboration does not hide an arrogant style with M. Cahier, however and, in a way, it suits his way of doing things, for his cooking is just as he describes it: unencumbered by needless elaboration, choosing little more than classical pairings and time-honoured collaborations.

With shellfish, he will extract the natural sweetness in cooking and then concoct a suitable sauce, perhaps the narcotic alliance of brandy and cream with scallops, or something smooth and herby for a feuilleté of seafood. With fresh fish, his sense of simplicity is perfect and fillets of john dory, or whatever has been landed in the harbour that day, are cooked just so, retaining vigour and freshness which his use of herbs agreeably accentuates. Cahier is an assured cook, so assured, indeed, that he has no need to be verbose or gimmicky, whether he is assembling toothy moules marinière as a starter or a super-duper tarte tatin for dessert. He simply lets the ingredients and his professional transformation of them do all the talking.

Open 7.30pm-9.30pm Tue-Sat
Closed 3 weeks in Feb
Average Price: dinner £18
Credit Cards: Visa, Access/Master
10% Service Charge
Wine Licence
Wheelchair Access
Children — welcome (but no special menu offered)
Vegetarians must give a day's notice
On the main street in Schull, near the entrance to the harbour.

THE CRAWFORD GALLERY CAFÉ

Emmet Place, Cork, Co Cork Tel: (021) 274415
Fern Allen

One suspects it is somewhat frustrating, being the curator of the Crawford. Every day, droves of people pile through those impressively heavy doors, and an onlooker might imagine that the citizens of Cork were the most art-fixated folk this side of the Guggenheims and Charles Saatchi.

Oh dear. Those droves are not headed towards the art on walls or the plinths, but to the art on the plate. Fern Allen's restaurant occupies a truly lovely room, and you find here some truly lovely food, meltingly maternal, surreptitiously soulful. For lunch, some potato and herb soup, a brewy bowl that, you might fancy, almost cares about you and wants to restore your equilibrium. Some brill from Ballycotton Bay, with a serenely smooth hollandaise flecked with dill, accompanied by duchesse potatoes, a few crisp sprouts. Some home-made lemonade. A cup of coffee and a sweet biscuit. Art? someone might ask. Art, indeed.

Open 10.30am-5.30pm Mon-Sat, 6.30pm-9.30pm Wed-Fri
Closed Xmas and bank holidays
Average Price: lunch £7, dinner £15-£20
Credit Cards: Visa, Access/Master
No Service Charge
Wine Licence
Wheelchair Access (3 steps to gallery, thereafter flat)
Children — welcome
Vegetarian menu always available
Cork city centre, on the ground floor of the gallery.

DUNWORLEY COTTAGE RESTAURANT ★
Dunworley, Butlerstown, Co Cork Tel: (023) 40314

For those who love Katherine Noren's restaurant, it is unimaginable — impossible! — to consider that there might be folk who would not regard it as one of the greatest restaurants in the country, one of the most singular restaurants in the north of Europe, a wild card, a one-off. The disciples of Dunworley point eagerly and hungrily to its protean perfection, go quiet with awe at the purity of taste which every morsel of the food Asa Helmerson cooks here exhibits so perfectly, go wide-eyed in explanation at the elemental wildness in which the restaurant is located and how this is so decisive an influence on the foods which Mrs Noren collects and cooks. If there should, ideally, be a dialogue between every restaurant and the environment from which it sources and secures its foodstuffs, then Dunworley expresses that dialogue with the finesse of a Shakesperian ode.

Dunworley hand-raised pork is peerless; the veal used in the blanquette is surely one of the greatest things you have ever eaten in your life; the smoked salmon from Frank Hedermann can have a strong-willed stomach weak with delight; the cured salmon with some salmon roe in the cream is staggering; the smoked mussels seem out-of-this-world with their etherealised allure. There is nothing to be said about the cured fish Mrs Noren prepares, and which she serves with icy glasses of aquavit, save that if you have eaten it, then you can die happy.

Some folk don't like Dunworley. They find the furnishings too stark, too simple, they find the tastes too unsubdued, too urgent. The acolytes like the Shaker plainness in the design, for it doesn't distract from the food, and the acolytes say that there is nowhere else like Dunworley and that the food is unforgettable. And that is certainly true.

Open summer lunch 1pm-3pm, dinner from 6.30pm Wed-Sun
Closed Nov and Jan-early Mar
Average Price: a la carte from £6, dinner £20
Credit Cards: Visa, Access/Master, Amex, Diners
No Service Charge
Restaurant Licence (plus bring your own for £2 corkage)
Wheelchair Access
Children — highchairs, half portions
Recommended for Vegetarians
The restaurant is well signposted as you drive from Timoleague.

HEIR ISLAND RESTAURANT ➡

Island Cottage, Roaringwater Bay, Co Cork Tel: (028) 38102
John Desmond & Ellmary Fenton

If you wanted to do something unlikely, then how about this. Open a
small restaurant. On an island. The sort of island which means that
your customers, having made their way down to the far reaches of
West Cork in the first place, must then also make a boat journey
across in order to eat. To complete this crazy idea, offer only one
set menu each evening. No choice, no matter who is dining.
John Desmond and Ellmary Fenton's Island Cottage, on Heir Island off
the coast of West Cork, does all these things. It represents something so
utterly unlikely and so obstinately awkward, it was surely assured of
success and, indeed, the inaccessibility of Heir Island has proven to be
one of its greatest attractions.
For one thing, the boat journey across is so entrancing that you find
yourself talking in Moon-in-June couplets even before you have hit the
island: the sky, the sea, the instant comradeship with the other diners.
This is a Fred and Ginger affair, a Cary Grant and Joan Fontaine special.
And, as for the food, there are important precedents for John
Desmond's refusal to cook a broad menu. Alice Waters in San
Francisco's famed Chez Panisse offers only one dinner menu each
evening. In London, Sally Clarke does the same. The only important
rule about restaurant cooking, ultimately, is that it should be good,
and on this Mr Desmond scores handsomely. Skill and sympathy are
bedfellows in his work, so much so that on one visit here the entire
congregation of eaters broke into spontaneous applause when he shyly
peeked his head out of the kitchen. After one visit to Island Cottage, it
took us, fully, four or five days before we had calmed down enough in
order to try to achieve some balance, some critical perspective on the
evening, could manage something other than purple prose. Abandon
all rationality, ye who take the boat to Heir Island.

Open for bookings of eight minimum (less will be accommodated if the restaurant has
a booking) Mon-Sun in season (ask details of boat times)
Closed Nov-Apr
Average Price: dinner £16
No Service Charge. Boatman charges approx. £3 per head.
No Credit Cards
Wine Licence
No Wheelchair Access　　Children — no facilities
No Vegetarian menu
The best boat to get leaves from Cunnamore. Driving from Skibbereen to Ballydehob,
turn left at Church Cross (signposted to Heir Island). Keep going until the road ends
at the Cunnamore car park.

ISAAC'S BRASSERIE
MacCurtain Street, Cork, Co Cork Tel: (021) 503805
Canice Sharkey

Isaac's, at lunchtime, with the big tall room light and bright, is a splendid place, and Canice Sharkey's food will be full of suggestions to inspire the appetite: some shellfish soup with a soft pink rouille served alongside; some colourful fresh pasta ribboned on the plate and swathed with fresh asparagus and parmesan; a swaggering chicken pie under a crown of pastry; a charcoal-grilled steak sandwich served with big fat chips. The simplicity and informality of the food suits a simple, speedy bite, but its correctness and stylishness will suit a luridly long excursion with plenty of white wine, a conference with friends that tails off somewhere late in the afternoon.

At dinnertime, the catholicity of Mr Sharkey's cooking always seems apt and able to offer just what you feel like eating, whether that be true tasting crab cakes in the American style, a stew of beans with Clonakilty black pudding, maybe a subtle lamb curry or some of his splendid pasta. Such an international array of dishes on one menu may suggest that the food will be no more than ersatz, but Mr Sharkey is a self-controlled cook — indeed, Isaac's needs his discipline, for no one else in the kitchen can concoct this food with as much aplomb and sureness as the man himself — and the flavours in his food are as buzzy and happy as the atmosphere in the lovely dining room.

Open 10am-10.30pm Mon-Sat, 6.30pm-9pm Sun
Closed Xmas
Average Price: lunch £5-£7, dinner £10-£12
Credit Cards: Visa, Access/Master
No Service Charge
Wine Licence
Wheelchair Access
Children — half price menu
Vegetarian options always available
Cork city centre, north of the river.

THE IVORY TOWER RESTAURANT ➤

The Exchange Buildings, 35 Princes Street, Cork, Co Cork Tel: (021) 274665
Seamus O'Connell

The most important thing to be said about Seamus O'Connell's cooking
is that he can do things other people couldn't manage to do in a month
of Sundays and, with the stuff they can do, he can usually do it better.
Here is a cook who might, fairly, be described as a virtuoso, with all
the excitements — and the problems — which that description entails.
The excitements which this virtuoso can spin out of the kitchen are
heady and intense, the menus utterly thrilling just to look at, never
mind to actually eat. There might be mackerel escabeche provençale,
then wild rabbit with coriander and prunes and a millfeuille of cherries
to complete a dazzling dinner
For Sunday lunch, the agony of choosing between mussel chowder
with peppers and walnuts or spinach and blue cheese filo parcels is just
the beginning of your difficulties: will it then be a lentil and spinach
stuffed yellow pepper, or a leg of lamb with a tarragon cream sauce?
Then surely it will have to be apple and caramel tarte tatin? The
chocolate rum cake? An apricot tart with sorbets? Problems! Problems!
The difficulty with virtuoso cooking, of course, is that any slight slip
in this standard of intense creativity seems greater than it might
elsewhere. No matter: Mr O'Connell's tight-rope act works without
a safety net, like Icarus ascending on beautiful foolish arms.
'I would like to open people's minds about food. I find there is no one
who is really surprising people with cooking, challenging people with
new ideas', says Mr O'Connell. A meal in The Ivory Tower, itself just a
simple room upstairs, is a surprise and a challenge, an assortment of
new ideas which suggests you have encountered student and guru,
teacher and preacher.

Open noon-4pm Mon-Sat, 6.30pm-11pm Wed-Sun
Closed Xmas week and 2 weeks in March
Average Price: lunch £5-£10, dinner £15-£20
No Credit Cards
No Service Charge
Wine Licence
No Wheelchair Access
Children — high chair
Recommended for Vegetarians
Princes Street leads off St Patrick's Street.

LETTERCOLLUM HOUSE ➡ £

Timoleague, Co Cork Tel: (023) 46251
Con McLoughlin

It may seem somewhat less than professional to use the example of a single lunch to describe the merits and manifestations of a restaurant. But, very occasionally, one has a single meal in a restaurant, with some friends to share it with and that easy-going sort of day which begins with a pint in the pub and stretches on into the afternoon, and the experience is so magical that it is hard, perhaps impossible, to forget the happiness which good food in good surroundings engendered.
One Sunday lunch, in the dining room in Lettercollum, there were tables of wrinkly old folk beside tables lined up with toddlers, babies in carry-tots, quartets of the chattering classes, local families relaxing in the afternoon balm of the dining room and, to complete the picture, outside there was a stretched Mercedes limousine with a be-hatted chauffeur, while inside the extended family who occupied it were getting on delightedly with the business of a birthday party.
If the atmosphere was mighty on the day, then so was the food. Having the benefit of a walled garden which gives him most of the organic vegetables and herbs he needs underpins the confident flavours which Con McLoughlin's food offers, allowing him to offer a true cuisine paysanne. A peppery and reviving courgette soup; salad composé bright with garden trueness; roast leg of lamb with perfect bedfellows in the shape of fresh garlic and tarragon; a daube of beef soulful and mouth-melting. The small details you want for a Sunday lunch — crisp roast spuds, spoonful desserts, teasingly aromatic coffee — were perfect and, at the end, we protested that they were not charging half enough for such taste-addled food. Time stood still. A perfect lunch.

Open 7.30pm-9.30pm Tue-Sun, 1.30pm-3.30pm Sun (check times out of season)
Closed Xmas
Average Price: lunch £10, dinner £17.50
Credit Cards: Visa, Access/Master, Diners
No Service Charge
Wine Licence
Wheelchair Access
Children — high chairs and half portions
Recommended for Vegetarians
Just outside Timoleague and clearly signposted.

LONGUEVILLE HOUSE AND PRESIDENT'S RESTAURANT ★

Mallow, Co Cork Tel: (022) 47156 Fax: 47459
William, Jane and Aisling O'Callaghan

William O'Callaghan is an outrageously talented cook, a chef whose culinary fluencies seem to know no boundary. A happy year spent working in England with Raymond Blanc 'opened my eyes', says Mr O'Callaghan. 'He gets into it, he gets into the food, he doesn't keep himself apart from anything. A lot of chefs just do it and get it out, but he gets involved in it. So that involvement is what I want'. This involvement means that with each dish Mr O'Callaghan seeks the inherent flavours of the food and in the case of Longueville this has particular resonance, for the house is almost self-sufficient and here one eats the food of the area in the area. Perhaps the best way, then, to enjoy Longueville is to opt for the Surprise Menu. A charlotte of Longueville lamb fillets and baby courgettes set in a tomato concassé begins, the marbling of the meat and the vegetables perfect, the sweet flavours offset by a herb vinaigrette. Then a ravioli of prawns with the juices scented with basil, and pan fried fillets of black sole with a gâteau of garden vegetables. Pause for lemon sorbet, then breast of farmyard duck with a ginger and coriander sauce accompanied by a potato straw cake, and desserts begin with a stunning hot lemon mousse, and conclude with a blackcurrant sorbet wrapped in a pancake and gratinated with a sabayon.

This sublime indulgence is remarkably balanced, and the courses follow seamlessly, with nothing discordant allowed to interrupt the procession. The use of herbs is liberal, but they play much more than a supporting role, strongly influencing the final flavour of the dishes. Finally, Mr O'Callaghan can cook anything: the ravioli is as expert as the fish is expertly simple: the lemon mousse as torchily exciting as the charlotte. And that is the key to his magic: he is excited by food, excited by cooking, and the result is delirious.

Open to non residents for lunch and dinner, if pre booked
Closed late Dec-early Mar
Average Price: lunch £15, dinner £26
Credit Cards: Visa, Access/Master, Amex, Diners
No Service Charge
Full Pub Licence
Wheelchair Access
Children — high chair
Recommended for Vegetarians
3 miles west of Mallow on the N72 to Killarney.

LOVETT'S

Churchyard Lane, Well Road, Douglas, Co Cork Tel: (021) 294909 Fax: 508568 Dermod & Margaret Lovett

A certain degree of misconception surrounds Dermod Lovett's eponymous restaurant.

Because it attracts scores of businessmen, mostly hell-bent on boozy lunches, one might imagine it as a dreadfully formal sort of place, keen to cater only for the credit card and expense account set. Because it has one of the most select and intelligent wine lists in the country, one might further imagine it as a stuffed-shirt sort of operation, the kind of place that might scoff if you asked for a glass of Aussie Chardonnay. In fact, Lovett's manages the awkward trick of successfully catering for almost everybody, without any sense of conflict, and it is an easy and enjoyable thing to pick and choose the type of Lovett's you wish to enjoy. At lunchtime the food in the bar is informal, but carefully attended to and charmingly served. If you wish for something more formal, then the food in the restaurant is perfect for a light lunch, for the fish cookery is always well achieved.

In the evening, the menu is more ambitious, but there is still nothing precious about the place, and one really should endeavour to make the most of Lovett's massive and select wine list. Mr Lovett's concern makes this a good location to splash out on something aristocratically bibulous, secure in the knowledge that the wines will have been cosseted with care, and secure in the knowledge Mrs Lovett's food will partner your bottle perfectly.

Open 12.30pm-2pm, 7pm-10pm Mon-Fri, 7pm-10pm Sat
Closed Xmas and bank holidays
Average Price: lunch £14.50, dinner £21
Credit Cards: Visa, Access/Master, Amex, Diners
12.5% Service Charge
Full Pub Licence
Wheelchair Access to restaurant and bar, but not toilets
Children — welcome if well behaved
Vegetarian menu of three choices always available
From Cork take Route 609 to Douglas. Turn onto the Well Road, and the restaurant is on your left.

MICHAEL'S BISTRO

4, Mardyke Street, Cork, Co Cork Tel: (021) 275333
Michael Clifford

Whilst superstar chefs in other countries have begun to re-discover the
pleasures and verities of simple cooking — one thinks of Jacques Cagna
and Michel Rostang in Paris, Alice Waters with her pizza restaurant in
San Francisco's Chez Panisse, even Marco Pierre White with his Chelsea
Canteen as a counterpoint to the voluptuousness of his Restaurant, Irish
cooks have also begun to seek an outlet for that eternal desire to do frites
and steak haché, omelettes and pasta, lamb shanks with flageolets.
In Kenmare, Maura Foley moved her skills towards a simpler, less saucy
scheme of things. In Clifden, Paddy Foyle scaled down the complexity
and scaled up the humour when he opened Destry Rides Again. In
Dublin, the Elephant & Castle has seen no need to alter its modus
operandi by a jot, whilst Colin O'Daly's tenure in Roly's Bistro elides
ever on as that restaurant's formula proves enduringly successful.
Now, wisely and just at the perfect time, Michael Clifford has taken the
same step, and used his christian name to open a second eponymous
restaurant, Michael's, sister ship to Clifford's, thereby further swelling
the riches of the culinary capital of Ireland. There are now so many places
to eat in Cork city for lunch and dinner that a day trip poses intractable
problems, simply in trying to decide just where it is that you want to go.
Many folk will go to Michael's, of course, for the Clifford culinary
signatures — happy staff, motivated cooking, true flavours, good value,
a devotion to the enjoyment of food — are nothing less than a blueprint
for bistro bliss. Under the orchestration of Paddy Kennedy, expect
hamburgers of crubeens with black pudding, a casserole of homemade
sausages, a ravioli of chicken with Milleens cheese, and thrilling re-
interpretations of Irish stew and bacon and cabbage. Black and white
styling, and the integral intimacy of the small room, seals the savoir faire
of Michael's.

Open noon-3pm, 6pm-10.30pm Mon-Sat (closed Sat lunch)
Closed Xmas Day
Average Price: meals £10
Credit Cards: Visa, Access/Master
No Service Charge
Wine Licence
Wheelchair Access
Children — welcome
Varied Vegetarian dishes served
A minute's walk from Jury's: turn left, then right and at the first set of traffic lights
you will see the restaurant.

THE OYSTERCATCHER RESTAURANT →

Oysterhaven, Co Cork Tel: (021) 770822
Sylvia & Bill Patterson

Bill Patterson cooks with a self-assurance that puts one in mind of the way in which Jean Renoir made movies. Confident, rhythmic, capable of establishing his own milieu in the course of a meal, he exhibits an enormous culinary fluency in everything he cooks.

But the movies finds another echo in Mr Patterson's food, for he subverts the great thriller cliché of Hollywood — start with an earthquake and build up to a climax!, a rule which many chefs observe with the structure of a meal — preferring instead to begin with a bang and to then slowly and sinuously wind a meal down so that it ends with a whimper, of delight.

A Trio of Rock Oysters on a bed of Angel Hair Pasta topped with a Raspberry Sauce is infernally pyrotechnical, yet the dish impresses most with its cleanness of taste. A similarly cosmopolitan invention, Hot Smoked Wild Irish Salmon on a Blini with Leek Sauce, features thickly-cut slices of Ummera salmon on blinis of ethereal finesse, a leek sauce picking up an echo of the greenness from the accompanying salad.

The grandness of this food comes as much from its comforting succour as it does from the high notes you expect from smoked salmon and oysters, venison and duck. Marinated Local Venison on a Pepper Sauce is judiciously sweet and tender, Breast of Landes Duck with a Herb and Sherry Vinegar Sauce is simple and assured, effortlessly understated.

Desserts like Prunes in Armagnac with Vanilla Ice-Cream or Crème Brûlée are true to their nature, prepared according to classic strictures. After the shock of the starters, the progression into subtle main courses and through a fine cheeseboard into these comforting desserts is beautifully judged. The dinner menu — there is no à la carte selection aside from the broad range of choices on the table d'hôte — concentrates on describing the source of the ingredients, the wine list is excellent, service is perfect, the experience is blissful.

Open 7pm-9.30pm Mon-Sat
Closed mid Jan-mid Feb
Average Price: dinner £21.95
Credit Cards: Visa, Access/Master
10% Service Charge on parties of six or more
Wine Licence
Wheelchair Access
Children — every effort made to accommodate them
Recommended for Vegetarians if given 24 hrs notice
Follow signs for Oysterhaven, and the restaurant is just on your left before you go over the bridge into the village.

CAFÉ PARADISO

16 Lancaster Quay, Western Road, Cork, Co Cork Tel: (021) 277939
Denis Cotter

Denis Cotter's Café is a simply decorated big room, facing immediately
onto the street, filled with tables and chairs, with a simple counter at
the end from which waitresses fetch food, and a cooking area into
which you can expectantly peer to see the cook at work.

For what Mr Cotter does and for the way Mr Cotter cooks, this space
proves apposite and appropriate. His cooking is quiet and effective,
with little in the way of frills and needless gestures, but it is annotated
by a broad vision and underpinned by a serious devotion to good
flavours. He is also a harbinger of what is to come, for Café Paradiso is
a vegetarian restaurant, but the carnivore who eats here will not find
that there is anything missing from the food. This cuisine is complete
of and unto itself, and Café Paradiso marks the beginning of genuine
creativity within vegetarian cookery in Ireland.

Mr Cotter has opened his style up to the influences of the New World:
a house soup elsewhere would be stodgy carrot, but here it has the
svelteness of coriander to lift its profile and, with a baked croissant
sandwich with brie, fresh and sun-dried tomatoes and salad sidled
into it, it makes for a superb lunch.

There may be a salad of wild and basmati rices or a lovely — though
ferociously peppery — leek and peppercorn tart. In the evening the menu
opens out: vegetable stir-fry in a hot and sour black bean sauce with
roasted cashews and fragrant rice; a gougere pastry ring filled with
Gabriel cheese, Thai cashew and tofu sandwich fritters; fresh spinach
tagliatelle with mushrooms in a red wine sauce; broccoli and blue cheese
filo pastry pie with a potato, aubergine and coriander stew. The desserts,
by Jacinta Cronin, are jaw-droppingly fine: Tia Maria iced cream
bombettes; butterscotch and walnut cheesecake; ginger sautéed pears
with iced mascarpone. Incidentally, it can appear in here, at times, that
smoking is compulsory: don't worry, it's not.

Open 10.30am-10.30pm (lunch 12.30pm-3.30pm, dinner 6.30pm-10.30pm) Tue-Sat
Closed Xmas week
Average Price: lunch £3-£5, dinner £10-£12
Credit Cards: Visa, Access/Master
No Service Charge
Wine Licence
Wheelchair Access to restaurant, but not to toilets
Children — half portions, high chairs, toys and books
Recommended for Vegetarians
Opposite Jury's hotel.

THE RECTORY

Glandore, Co Cork Tel: (028) 33072
Sean O'Boyle

Glandore is one of the most beautiful villages of south west Cork, but for the gastronome it has always been a place where the heart sinks: how could such a beautiful place exist with nowhere to stop and enjoy a meal.

The owners of the Marine Hotel have, at last, rectified this by opening up the three downstairs rooms of their own home, a high, wide, handsome and quite magnificent Georgian rectory with huge bay windows that they have re-decorated in glowing reds, greens and blues. Two Dublin chefs have been imported, and head chef Kieran Scully's food has all the signatures of modern styling — large plates, great fondness of colour, food presented in a very finished fashion. There can be fine moments in a meal: warm smoked salmon on a bed of leaves; an excellent breast of chicken which is stuffed with a mousse of its own liver; softly toothsome pheasant which is majestically sweet; wonderful ice creams on a crisp tuille basket.

When it works, the Rectory works very well, but there is still, perhaps, a little more confidence needed, a little more finishing, particularly with the vegetables which are unimaginative, the service — which needs to be more commanding — and the music, which is too effervescently poppy for such grand rooms. All this will come with time.

Open 7pm-9.30pm Mon-Sun (with limited hours and weekends only off season)
Closed Xmas
Average Price: dinner £21
Credit Cards: Visa, Access/Master, Amex
No Service Charge
Full Licence
Wheelchair Access
Children — no special facilities
Vegetarian meals on request
Signposted just as you enter Glandore village after turning off the main road at Leap.
There are two entrances.

SEAN NA MBADS

Ringabella, Minnane Bridge, Co Cork Tel: (021) 887397
Fiona McDonald

No signposts signal this out-of-the-way restaurant and pub near Carrigaline, but it's someplace worth hunting down. An old stone two-storey house, it's divided into a couple of bars with cattle market tall counters and captain's chair-type stools, a billiards room and a dining room lined from floor to low ceiling with books.

Whilst this might sound like an amateurish Big House dinner-party sort of a place, one look at the menu reveals that a professional touch is behind what was once a simple country pub and Alan Errington's cooking is assured. Mushrooms are stuffed with roasted shallots in a delicious blend where the two ingredients sympathise perfectly; goats cheese is souffléd and dressed with salad leaves and a hazle-nut dressing. Saddle of Rabbit is confidently roasted, a breast of Barbary duck given a port wine sauce and accompanied by a purée of leek and mushrooms. Brill is made into a mousse, then poached and served with mussels with a sauce studded with tomatoes and chives. The only difficulty with the menu, in fact, is the somewhat silly affectation whereby prices are spelt out with letters, rather than conventional and sensible numbers. The wine list is short, but the finer wines offered are interesting, with the Perrin family's lovely Chateau Beaucastel calling out for an order of autumnal meats. You can book a table but they don't, in fact, reserve them. Be warned that it is truly difficult to find Sean na mBads, so get details from them when calling.

Open 7pm-10.30pm Thur-Sun (bar open every day)
Closed Xmas Day, Good Fri
Average Price: dinner £17.50
Credit Cards: Visa, Access/Master
No Service Charge
Full Pub Licence
Wheelchair Access
Children — welcome in bar
Vegetarian meals on request
6 miles from Carrigaline, 2 miles from Roberts Cove: about 3 miles past Minnane Bridge heading to Roberts Cove, take a left to Ringabella and look out for a cul-de-sac, a cluster of houses and twin forks.

SHIRO JAPANESE DINNER HOUSE ➡

Ahakista, Co Cork Tel: (027) 67030
Kei and Werner Pilz

There are only two tables in the Shiro Japanese Dinner House, each
in separate rooms and each available only to a single party each
evening. There is only Kei Pilz and her husband Werner to cook
and to serve, and their food is only quite extraordinary, something
that almost demands the realm of the sexual vocabulary to attempt
adequate expression of the pleasure it gives.

In the Shiro, an ideal of heightened, almost narcotic, delight is pursued
and orchestrated by Kei Pilz by means of a sinuous procession of
dishes, each of them separate but, ultimately, sympathetic and
harmonious. The achievement of this culinary alchemy is conceived
as operating on a broad canvas and in a slow and steady time-flow,
with that final sense of satisfaction, that pinnacle of pleasure, arising
only at the conclusion of a meal. One thinks of equivalents from other
disciplines — a Mozart sonata or a late Beethoven quartet, the depth
of an abstract by Rothko — for there can seem to be too few
equivalents among the culinary arts.

With every delicious morsel parcelled exquisitely, the procession
parades food that is a delight to the eye — the filigree fans of tempura
served on a wooden board, tenderly carved vegetables, a brown
Windsorish sui-mono with tofu and cabbage greens hidden in the soup
— and a delight to the palate — smoky tea-leaved sea weed as part of
Azuke-Bachi, supple sashimi of mackerel, salmon and squid. Through
the course of the evening, this seems to motivate and arouse, and
ultimately exhaust, every sense in the body, and to touch upon the soul.

Open 7pm-9pm Tue-Sat
Closed Xmas and Jan
Average Price: dinner £33
Credit Cards: Visa, Access/Master, Amex (payment by credit card incurs an additional
charge of 5%)
No Service Charge
Wine Licence
No Wheelchair Access
Children — no facilities
Recommended for Vegetarians
Signposted from the Cork-Bantry road and from the village of Durrus.

TRA AMICI

Dromkeal, Coomhola Road, Ballylickey, Co Cork Tel: (027) 50235
Sean Vail

In Tra Amici, the food amounts to an 'episode for the senses', to use an expression of the great Italian cook and writer Marcella Hazan. Be warned: one episode is never enough. You will wish to make Tra Amici into a long running series for the senses.

The food in Tra Amici looks, superficially, simple: Spaghetti al Pesto, Carpaccio all' Albese, Pollo alla Cacciatora, the familiar dishes we associate with Italian cuisine, but Sean Vail cooks these foods the way an Italian would cook them at home in Italy and he achieves, on occasion, nothing less than a transcendent, mysterious magic.

His Spaghetti al Pesto is the perfect alliance of soft noodles and a sauce which sinuously elides its subtle basil and cheese tastes with the pasta. The tastes are simple, correct, sympathetic, and elusively magical, and they are to be found throughout a meal: Vermicelli with clams, soft thimbles of gnocchi with a red sauce, delicate veal that disappears in the mouth, a sublime baked cheesecake.

Mr Vail talks modestly about his cooking, describing it as 'Occasion Cooking'. 'Italians would cook these type of dishes on special occasions: gnocchi is something the family sits down and makes for something like a wedding, or for Easter', he says.

Whilst this explanation signals the general direction of the Italian food Mr Vail cooks, away from trattoria rubbish and firmly to the heart of true Italian cooking, it does little to suggest the heights of sublimity to which his cooking can ascend. The real key to his work may lie in the admission that, 'We look at the restaurant as an extension of our home: I would treat people in the dining room the same as if I were entertaining someone in my house'.

Open 7pm-10pm Mon-Sat
Closed 1 Oct-1 Apr
Average Price: dinner £17.50-£22.50
Credit Cards: Visa, Access/Master
No Service Charge
Wine Licence
Wheelchair Access (incl disabled toilet)
Children — special children's menu on request
Vegetarian options always served, special requests always considered
Signposted at the Ballylickey Bridge.

CASTLE MURRAY HOUSE
Dunkineely, Co Donegal Tel: (073) 37022
Thierry Delcros

Thierry Delcros's restaurant has been one of the most inspiring
success stories in recent years. Having quietly worked his way around
this place and that, gifting other people's restaurants and hotels with
the benefit of his exquisitely attuned skills, M. Delcros and his wife
Claire opened Castle Murray at the end of 1989.
The news of their good food spread like wildfire, not just in Donegal — a
county where, on all too many occasions, you would wish that it would be
possible that you could eat the view, for the view would be delicious and
dinner would not — but also across the border into the North. The reasons
for this success are instantly recognisable: a lack of pretentiousness, superb
food at good prices and the ability, because those prices are so keen, to stay
overnight in one of their rooms and thus make a decent night of it. This is
the simple concept of the Restaurant with Rooms, seen here at its very best.
M. Delcros' cooking remains very, devotedly, concentratedly French
but, like the cooking of Dunworley Cottage in County Cork, for
example, where the influence is Swedish, his work proves the perfect
marriage between Irish ingredients — wild game birds, fresh fish and
shellfish, bio-dynamically grown vegetables, fresh eggs from run-
around chickens — and the precise strictures of classic techniques.
He doesn't innovate very much — there will be pâtés, effete soups, fish
with sauces, meats with sauces, and you can have a dinner as simple as
onion soup, then a grilled sirloin steak and some ices to finish if you wish,
but it is in the extraction of flavour and the respect for balance in a dish
which is his signature: this cooking tastes right, from Tournedos façon
Rossini to Braised Brill with Leeks, from McSweyne's Bay Blue Lobster to
Fresh Pasta au Poisson. On a busy night service can get a little strung-out,
but there is always the startlingly beautiful view to regard, and this is food
worth waiting for.

Open 7pm-9.30pm ('till 10pm Sat and Sun) Mon-Sun, 1pm-2.30pm Sun Closed Xmas
and Mon-Wed off season
Average Price: lunch £13, dinner £16-£20
Credit Cards: Visa, Access/Master, Diners
No Service Charge
Full Licence
Wheelchair Access
Children — welcome, no special menu
Recommended for Vegetarians
Vegetarian meals available on request
Signposted just after the village of Dunkineely.

RESTAURANT ST JOHN'S

Fahan, Inishowen, Co Donegal Tel: (077) 60289
Reggie Ryan

Do not disparage the virtue of certainty.
Phil McAfee's cooking in Restaurant St. John may not consist of
concoctions, inventions and improvisations from the cutting edge of
the culinary world. He may not wish to dabble a toe in the waters of the
Pacific Rim, may never have read a book about blue corn and chocolate
combinations — as per the Navajo Indians, or the Incas, or his great-aunt,
or Fanny and Johnny on a bender, or whoever — but he knows what his
customers like and appreciate and want, and he knows how to deliver it
to them.
This is the secret of Reggie Ryan's enduring restaurant. It is not an
ephemeral place, as are so many others in the restaurant world.
Instead, it endures, year in and year out, by virtue of doing what they
do and doing it right. They don't change just because others change,
any alterations done here will be done slowly and carefully, and
revisions thought about for a long time before being put into practice.
So, expect stuffed local mussels, pork fillet with a port wine sauce,
chicken breast with tarragon cream, brill with lemon butter. And
expect careful service and a splendid wine list: Grange Hermitage,
Palmer, Latour and Clos De La Roche if you have the money to
blow-out, but lots of other fine, gluggable stuff at very good prices.

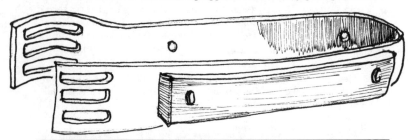

Open 7pm-10pm Tue-Sat
Closed Xmas Day, Good Fri
Average Price: dinner £20
Credit Cards: Visa, Access/Master, Amex, Diners
10% Service Charge
Restaurant Licence
Wheelchair Access
Children — no facilities
Varied Vegetarian Menu served each evening
On the left hand side of the road as you enter Fahan, and clearly signposted.

ADRIAN'S

3 Abbey Street, Howth, Co Dublin Tel & Fax: (01) 391696
Adrian and Catriona Holden

It probably seems glib to describe the dishes Catriona Holden cooks
in Adrian's, a nifty little place in Howth which she runs with her Dad,
as 'moreish'. But, if it is glib, it is also accurate.

What else can you say about a place where, on a blustry Monday
lunchtime in January, one bloke, otherwise moon-in-Juneing with his
paramour, asks for an extra soupçon of soup. 'Like some more bread?',
Adrian Holden asks a pair of French folk. Yes, indeed they would like
some more of that deliciously doughy onion bread, that savoury olive
bread, those pert little white rolls with their crisp sesame tops.

The cause of this happiness is a young woman who looks like a teenager
and cooks with the vitality of an adolescent. On a first visit to Adrian's,
we asked what the chicken and tomato on garlic toast with glazed cheese
was like. 'Really yummy', said Ms Holden. And the mushroom and ginger
soup? 'Really hearty', said Ms Holden. She was right, both times.

Her skills enjoy a broad template: koulibiaca with a sorrel sauce; a
cornucopia of squid, rabbit casserole with little onions, haunch of
venison with kale, and she manages to prime each dish so that the
flavours are clambering out.

Ms Holden may appear unduly youthful, but there is a wisdom in both
her culinary and her business approach which is fit for someone far
beyond her years. You trust her judgement, trust her savvy, trust her
desire to do her best, you trust, above all, the fact that she understands
food as a creative art. The only way you will find yourself complaining
in Adrian's will be if, Heaven forbid, they should run out of something,
and you can't adopt your doe eyes and plead, please, for some more.

Open 12.30pm-3pm Mon-Sat, 6pm-9.30pm Mon-Sun ('till 8pm Sun)
Closed 25-26 Dec, Good Fri
Average Price: lunch £6.50-£7.90, dinner £16
Credit Cards: Visa, Access/Master, Amex, Diners
No Service Charge
Wine Licence
No Wheelchair Access (but no problem to help)
Children — welcome (discuss when booking)
Vegetarians need to give advance notice
At the end of Howth village, past the pier, where the road broadens out, Adrian's is
just a short stroll up the hill.

AYUMI-YA JAPANESE RESTAURANT

Newpark Centre, Newtownpark Avenue, Blackrock, Co Dublin
Tel: (01) 283 1767
Akiko Hoashi

The parent of the Ayumi-Ya Steakhouse in Dublin city, and one of the longest established restaurants in the county, the Ayumi-Ya continues to move through the years with grace and the promise of good food. Mrs Hoashi's food is as ornamented and as fine as one expects of Japanese cooking, whether you choose the Teppan-Yaki tables and have the food cooked immediately in front of you on hot plates, or if you decide to go native, sit on the floor and enjoy the calming service by the waitresses.

The set menus are excellent value for money, but sometimes it is fun to allow the restaurant to compose a menu for you — they even suggest that first-timers choose the Omakase-Menu, where the chefs select the food — and to indulge in a succession of sublime and sinuous and sympathetic dishes: tempura with its clamouring batter, tofu with its mellow indifference sharpened by deep-frying or mixed with sesame oil, shabu-shabu of thinly sliced beef washed in broth with grated radish. On an ideal evening, the flow of flavours will be as seamless as the sense of pleasure this food can engender, a sense of pleasure which everyone in the Ayumi-Ya works hard to create.

Open 7pm-11pm Mon-Sat, 6pm-10pm Sun
Closed Xmas, Good Fri, New Year's Day
Average Price: dinner £13.95-£14.95
Credit Cards: Visa, Access/Master, Amex, Diners
10% Service Charge
Restaurant Licence
Wheelchair Access to restaurant but not toilet
Children — welcome before 8.30pm, children's platter £6.95
Recommended for Vegetarians
At the Blackrock end of Newtownpark Avenue, amongst the small group of shops set back from the road by a small car park.

AYUMI-YA JAPANESE STEAKHOUSE

132 Lwr Baggot Street, Dublin 2 Tel: (01) 622 0233 Fax: 662 0221
Akiko and Yoichi Hoashi

You can fall in love with the food in the Ayumi-Ya, and find you crave
it as much as a lover craves the company of another. These tastes are
so tactile and satisfying, so intelligently realised, that they overturn our
conception of Japanese food as something cool, something remote.
This is friendly, lovable food.

The 'steaks' are Teppan steaks, and refer to the manner in which they are
cooked — over a hot iron griddle — rather than the beef, chicken, prawn,
salmon or vegetable that you select, and there is a Kushi-age menu: meat,
veg or seafood threaded onto skewers, breadcrumbed and deep fried.

The noodles, in great big deep bowls, need all the concentration they
are given by the clientele of Japanese businessmen who scoop and
slurp at the Soba, or buckwheat noodles, or the Udon, wheat noodles
which bask in bowls of soup garnished with batter and deep fried tofu.
Ayumi-Ya Ramen are egg noodles with caramel tasting roast pork and
slivers of raw root vegetable and there are two Japanese Pasta dishes of
pan fried noodles with stir fried vegetable or cod's roe.

If you cannot make it to eat in the Ayumi-Ya, take heart, and take a
Bento to go. 'The Bento began when people would go to the sumo, the
theatre, the kabuki', says Mrs Akiko Hoashi, 'It's portable food'.

The common feature of any Bento is rice — either boiled or fried — but
from that point on you can change any of the accompaniments:
Makunouchi Bento, in a large, rectangular box, may comprise boiled rice
with a little pickle on top, then some breaded and fried Prawn Ebifrai, a
little macaroni salad in dressing, some chicken Toritasuta-Age, a portion
of superb salted and grilled mackerel, a smattering of grilled leeks and
peppers and deliciously sweet butterbeans. Yakitori Bento offers skewered,
grilled pieces of chicken and onion, full of succulent, baleful tastes, and
the cleansing macaroni, sweet butterbeans and toothsome rice.

Open 12.30pm-2.30pm, 6pm-11.30pm Mon-Sat
Closed Xmas, New Year and Good Friday
Average Price: lunch £6.95-£9.95, dinner £9.95-£12.95
Credit Cards: Visa, Access/Master, Amex
10% Service Charge after 6pm
Wine Licence
No Wheelchair Access (though they are happy to carry wheel-chair bound customers
down the stairs)
Children — welcome until 8.30pm, high chair, children's platter £6.95
Recommended for Vegetarians
On the corner of Lwr Baggot Street and Lwr Pembroke Street, 5 mins walk from St
Stephen's Green.

CHINA-SICHUAN RESTAURANT

4 Lower Kilmacud Road, Stillorgan, Co Dublin Tel: (01) 288 4817
Fax: 288 0882
David Hui

Banish from your mind the vague memory of those beloved sizzling
dishes which you scoff, somewhat tipsy, on tipsy Saturday nights in
your local Chinese eating house, those fake concoctions of MSG and
culinary myopia.

Here, in David Hui's China-Sichuan, up in dreary, dull old Stillorgan,
you will find the counterpoint to that hideously compromised cooking
which we believe is Chinese food. In the China-Sichuan you find the
real thing: Hot & Sour Soup with a musky, coffee-odoured thrill of a
taste; pan fried dumplings with a fathom-black dipping sauce or in a
hot sauce with spicy chilli; chicken in a garlic sauce, the dish offering
endless nodes of viscous flavours; some monkfish with cashews
perhaps, the fish jumping with freshness and the tentacular cuts
putting you in mind of the roof of the Sydney Opera House.

With these, some voluptuously slinky Dan-Dan Mein noodles, or maybe
some clean boiled rice. Mr Li, the cook, rarely puts a cleaver wrong, and
the excitement of tastes which a dinner can deliver is one of the city's
delights. Expect to cough, occasionally, as the toxic charge of chillies hits
the back of the throat: apply Australian Chardonnay immediately. For
dessert, then, some gloriously cool almond bean curd, the taste like an
incredibly exotic marzipan, comes as a delicious surprise, the perfect
ending to a series of surprisingly accessible and yet delightfully authentic
tastes. Service is excellent, design is strictly unreconstructed over-the-top,
and this is an invaluable Chinese restaurant.

Open 12.30pm-2.30pm, 6pm-11pm Mon-Sun
Closed 25-27 Dec, Good Fri
Average Price: lunch £8-£10, dinner £16.50
Credit Cards: Visa, Access/Master, Amex
10% Service Charge
Wine Licence
Wheelchair Access to restaurant but not to toilet
Children — high chair available
Recommended for Vegetarians
Leave the Stillorgan dual carriageway after passing the Park Hotel, travelling south.
The restaurant is 100 yds from the Stillorgan Shopping Centre, on the Kilmacud
Road.

COOKE'S CAFÉ

14 South William Street, Dublin 2 Tel: (01) 679 0536/7/8
John Cooke

One must applaud the tremulous sense of theatre and nervy catwalk
fashionability which John Cooke's Café has brought to the business
of eating out in Dublin. Stylish and smack up-to-the-minute, the Café
quickly became the favoured rendezvous of the chattering classes, the
professional classes and, even, some ordinary decent folk who just
fancy some classy food served in an atmosphere bristling with brio.
With the benefit of experience, Cooke's has gradually overcome the
problems of boorish service which initially made it difficult to enjoy
the cooking and, whilst the staff are still not exactly the sort of folk
you'd welcome in if they rang your doorbell at 4 a.m., explaining that
their car has just run out of petrol and could they use your 'phone, they
are most usually polite and reasonably efficient in getting the job done.
This is important simply because John Cooke's food, with its sassy
tastes and its vibrant, well-informed use of colour and contrast, is food
that needs efficiency rather than ceremony. You don't linger over this
Cal-Ital cooking: you just get right in there and enjoy it: oily avocado
crossed with cool asparagus in a salad; roasted fillet of turbot with a
sauce of sweet butter and good oil; fettucine with smoked chicken
and field mushrooms in a delicate cream sauce which shows very
well-understood pasta cooking.

This food expresses a basic paradox, of course: peasant cuisine at high
prices to be enjoyed by the bourgeoisie, but then there is a paradox at
the heart of most every restaurant, and that at the centre of Cooke's
is no more unlikely than most others. It certainly doesn't make the
clientele self-conscious: all that worries them is the thought, the fear,
that whilst they are sitting here, some other darn restaurant has gone
and gotten more fashionable than Cooke's Café.

Open noon-6pm lunch, 6pm-11.30pm diner Mon-Sun
Closed Xmas, Good Fri and bank holiday lunches
Average Price: lunch £12, dinner £16-£20
Credit Cards: Visa, Access/Master, Amex, Diners
No Service Charge (12.5% on parties of 6 or more)
Wine Licence
Wheelchair Access (with advance notice only)
Children — welcome
Vegetarian options always available
At the back of the Powerscourt Townhouse Centre, on the corner at the zebra
crossing.

LE COQ HARDI

35 Pembroke Road, Dublin 4 Tel: (01) 668 4130/668 9070
John and Catherine Howard

The public perception of John Howard's restaurant, throughout its
long history, has always been of an archetypal bourgeois eating palace,
somewhere that slings culinary history right back to the days of César
Ritz and Auguste Escoffier, a restaurant which offers an uninterrupted
blow-out of classic cuisine and claret.

Yet, whilst this image can be true, and whilst the restaurant does like
to present itself as someplace where racehorse owners can land their
helicopters after a successful day at the Curragh before they begin to
fritter away their winnings on Haut-Brion and hâute cuisine — a
tureen of Dublin Bay Prawns scented with cognac, a millefeuille of
Irish salmon with a watercress butter sauce, a fricassée of monkfish
with black noodles, coq au vin in a pastry dome — there is actually
as much of the soft and ageless nature of French peasant cuisine to be
found here as there is cooking that is grandiose and verbose — long-
cooked oxtail braises, plump terrines of rabbit, chicken liver and leek,
hake with tomato, olives, olive oil and mashed potato, perfectly cooked
root vegetables, and the prices for set meals can be very fair. If you
do have a successful day at the Curragh, then the carte in the Coq will
soak up plenty of that easy-come money, and then there is one of the
great wine lists, just waiting to account for the rest.

Open 12.30pm-3pm Mon-Fri, 7pm-11pm Mon-Sat
Closed Xmas and 2 weeks in early Aug
Average Price: lunch £16, table d'hôte dinner £28
Credit Cards: Visa, Access/Master, Amex, Diners
12.5% Service Charge
Full Restaurant Licence
No Wheelchair Access
Children — no facilities
Varied Vegetarian Menu served each evening
On the right hand side when driving from Baggot Street towards Ballsbridge.

L'ECRIVAIN

112 Lr Baggot Street, Dublin 2 Tel: (01) 661 1919/088 596219
Fax: 661 0617
Derry & Sally-Anne Clarke

There are many reasons for the happily enduring success of the Clarkes'
L'Ecrivain restaurant, but chief amongst them is the fact that this
charming couple run a happy house, and when you are here you are
happy to be here and, when you leave you are unhappy to be leaving.
Derry Clarke's cooking works not just by virtue of clever sourcing of foods,
or confident skills in the kitchen. Not even thanks to a team of waiters and
waitresses who are so assured as to make you blink with delight.
No, Mr Clarke's food works because of the application of oodles of
common sense, a strain of common sense which ushers food out to the
customer in a pristine, lively state, full of taste and alert flavours. He will
dress oysters up in a bechamel with a little concasse of tomato then show
them the grill, and they will be hopping with flavour and vigour. He will
wait for an order, then pile a pillow of puff pastry with fresh vegetables
and sharpen the taste with fresh herbs to make a vegetarian delight. With
some mignons of beef, tarragon will coax on the flavour of beef which is
so tender it melts in the mouth like a meat chocolate.
Derry Clarke works in a tradition which, for many cooks, has come
to represent something of a culinary cul-de-sac: Cuisine Française is
often misrepresented in this country because cooks overcomplicate
the processes needed to prepare the food. Where Clarke wins out is
in waiting for an order, then springing into action to both begin and
finish a dish in the shortest possible time.
Having a small number of seats in this intimate restaurant allows him
the luxury of individual service, and while Clarke's staff could give
Masterclasses in the art of waiting on table, Mr Clarke himself could
give Masterclasses in the art of culinary common sense.

Open 12.30pm-2pm Mon-Fri, 6.30pm-11pm Mon-Sat
Closed Xmas and bank holidays
Average Price: lunch £13.50, dinner £22.95
Credit Cards: Visa, Access/Master, Amex, Diners
10% Service Charge (NB there is no service charge on any bottle of wine purchased
to the value of £20 or more)
Wine Licence
No Wheelchair Access
Children — no facilities (and no space!)
Full Vegetarian menu
In a basement on the corner of Baggot Street and Fitzwilliam Street.

ELEPHANT & CASTLE

18 Temple Bar, Dublin 2 Tel: (01) 679 3121
Liz Mee & John Hayes

Many have tried to copy the formula of the Elephant & Castle since
it opened, but none have succeeded in replicating the success of this
potent concoction. The failure of the copy-cats has lain, usually, in
their refusal to believe that there is, in fact, no formula behind this
simple, bare-boards'n't-shirts place. If there is no formula, however,
then perhaps there is a secret, and we might borrow an album title
from R.E.M., those aristocrats of rock'n'roll, and say that the secret
of the E&C is that it is Automatic For The People.

At any time of day or night, it serves the food you want and becomes
the place you want it to be. From 8 in-the-morning omelette breakfasts,
to a mid-morning gouter, to a pasta lunch with a girlfriend, maybe a
late afternoon pick-me-up tuna and guacamole sandwich or pre-theatre
chicken wings that have you licking your fingers right through the
performance, then onwards to a late night romantic rendezvous with
a loved-one, even post-pub burger and fried potatoes, perhaps a family
table for Sunday brunch.

All of the foods for all of these occasions can be found here. You can even,
indeed, eat in the E&C more than once a day, and find it is different, find
the style of food will have changed to suit the time of day.

The food is democratically priced, but never cheap: with these ingredients
it could never be. The basic menu has evolved little, if any, since it opened,
with innovation and experimentation coming from the daily specials,
which are always worth trying: lamb korma with relishes; fettucini with
chicken, shiitake mushrooms and asparagus, grilled fillet steak and rouille
served with herb mashed potato; Sichuan chicken with spicy stir-fried
noodles. Whatever you eat, it will be part of an ideal of service and
simplicity which announces itself as Automatic For The People.

Open 8am-11.30pm Mon-Thur, 8am-midnight Fri, 10.30am-midnight Sat, noon-
11.30pm Sun
Closed Xmas
Average Price: lunch £7-£10, dinner £15
Credit Cards: Visa, Access/Master, Amex, Diners
No Service Charge (except 10% for groups of 8 or more)
Wine Licence
Wheelchair Access
Children — welcome
Vegetarian options always available
In Dublin's Temple Bar, just on the south side of the River Liffey.

LES FRERES JACQUES
74 Dame Street, Dublin 2 Tel: (01) 679 4555
Jean-Jacques and Suzy Caillebet

There are plenty of judicious people who will select Les Freres Jacques as their favourite Dublin restaurant, and it is easy to see why. Walk down the little lane and through the door and the restaurant invites you in with that dim-lit light that suggests Parisian oyster bars or London clubs, suggests privacy and cosseting and pleasure.
For solo diners, Freres Jacques is just perfect: one day, a quiet spinster who peered through the window at the passers-by and a dog-collared priest who slugged cognacs were just some of the other soloists enjoying the effective, tasteful food and — most importantly — the uncondescending way in which it is served. And the food in Suzy and Jean-Jacques Caillebet's restaurant is almost always effective: a mussel and fennel soup rendered perfectly, and perfectly paired with bread flavoured with curry powder; some lobster ravioli with a fillet of turbot, and then an excellent vanilla bavarois. Sprigs of chervil decorate with simplicity and the fact that a bill can quickly add up hardly matters, though it is significant that straying away from the set menus can send the addition into the stratosphere, because the service charge is steep and, disappointingly, the waiting staff behave as if a tip is their God-given right. For special occasions, and especially for business lunching, the restaurant has that assured rhythm which derives from experience and confidence, but they don't let it slip into swagger, and their Gallic correctness has, over the years, been tempered with an Irish affability. It is a very French restaurant, but it is very definitely in Dublin.

Open 12.30pm-2.30pm Mon-Fri, 7.30pm-10.30pm Mon-Sat (Fri & Sat 'till 11pm)
Closed bank holidays
Average Price: lunch £13, dinner £20
Credit Cards: Visa, Access/Master, Amex, Diners
12.5% Service Charge
Restaurant Licence
No Wheelchair Access
Children — no facilities
Not suitable for Vegetarians
A few doors down from the Olympia Theatre on Dame Street, just across from Dublin Castle.

FURAMA CHINESE RESTAURANT

88 Donnybrook Road, Dublin 4 Tel: (01) 283 0522
Rodney Mak

One of the most pleasing aspects of the Furama is not just that their Chinese food is better than most other Chinese cooking in Dublin, but that their efforts to maintain authenticity and to cook true Chinese food are met by such an appreciative audience.

At weekends, the Furama is full of Dublin 4 types — weekend-access fathers spoiling their kids, rugby souls already tanked up on a few bevvies of beer, skinny women discussing their career curves — all enjoying the lush accents and sensual flavours which Freddie Lee's food delivers to the diner: King Prawn in spicy minced pork; roasted duck with its oily, smoky allure; black sole drunken style; green peppers stuffed with prawns in a garlic and black bean sauce. Indeed, The Furama exploits more varied techniques than most Chinese restaurants — and extends this to silver service at table when it comes to filleting fish — so there is much greater variety to be enjoyed, though the price is, appropriately, somewhat higher than other restaurants.

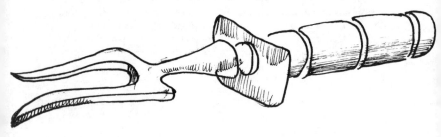

Open 12.30pm-2pm Mon-Fri, 6pm-11.30pm Mon-Sat, 1.30pm-11pm Sun
Open all year
Average Price: lunch £7.50, dinner £20
Credit Cards: Visa, Access/Master, Amex, Diners
10% Service Charge
Restaurant Licence
Wheelchair Access
Children — no facilities
Small selection of vegetarian dishes
Opposite Bective rugby ground, as you drive out of Donnybrook going south.

RESTAURANT PATRICK GUILBAUD

46 James Place, Baggot Street Lwr, Dublin 2 Tel: (01) 676 4192
Fax: 660 1546
Patrick Guilbaud

Patrick Guilbaud's eponymous restaurant is claustral in its pursuit of a classic idea of French food, pernickity as Martin Luther when it comes to the edicts of cooking.

'We are very classical', M. Guilbaud will tell you. 'All our sauces are the way they should be done. If we say we do a beurre blanc we do a beurre blanc, if we do a bearnaise we do a bearnaise, but the real way. We do everything the way it should be done'.

And this is true, and can make for fine eating, for you find you can recall years later the procession of tastes in a simple lunch, for example: duck liver mousse, brill with a buttery veloute sauce and some smoky asparagus, pistachio and dark chocolate gateau. The precision of tastes which chef Guillaume Lebrun can disclose from ingredients is never less than impressive and he can arrive at some magnificent alliances, though seasoning is always slightly on the aggressive side.

Yet Guilbaud's has evolved into a restaurant that is easy to admire yet impossible to love. You admire the hard-headed determination which created this purpose-built place, the well-drilled staff with their cloche synchronicity honed to the nth degree, the keenness of the prices for set menus. But admiring is one thing, and affection another, and Guilbaud's has never lost an air of cool distance, of hautiness, of arrogance. This makes it perfect for entertaining, for they get on with their work while you get on with yours and they never but never get in the way. But if you cherish humour, spontaneity, improvisation, cooking that comes from the heart rather than the head, then other cooks and other restaurants may be more beguiling.

Open 12.30pm-2pm, 7.30pm-10.15pm Tues-Sat
Closed 25-26 Dec and bank holidays
Average Price: set lunch £18.50, set dinner £25
Credit Cards: Visa, Access, Amex, Diners
15% Service Charge
Full Licence
Wheelchair Access
Children — high chairs
Function room available (seats 30)
Vegetarian dishes available on request (please give notice)
Behind the Bank of Ireland on Baggot Street.

THE IRISH FILM CENTRE

6 Eustace Street, Temple Bar, Dublin 2 Tel: (01 677 8788 Fax: 677 8755
Eddie Bates

The ideal of good food in a public space has been one of the guiding
lights of The Irish Film Centre, since this lean space opened its doors.
You can have a glass of beer and a sandwich downstairs, maybe a
muffin and a coffee, or you can pitch up the stairs to the lean space
of the restaurant, with its funky modernist seats and cat walk
arrangement of tables.

The food in the IFC is not just efficiently rendered, it also tastes very
true, very real. This is thanks to the clever simplicity of chef Eddie
Bates, a cook who never shows off and who manages to bring home the
true taste of a dish whether it hails from Morocco or Mullingar. He is
as good with Baba Ghanoush as with deep fried scampi, as comfortable
with Chinese Chicken and Bean Sprout pie — a provocative series of
soy-rich flavours bundled up in melting pastry — as with Vegetable
Strudel, the parcel of filo packed to bursting with pine nuts and set on
a light tomato sauce, with a tumble of couscous beside.

The rusticity of the food is an ironic counterpoint to the architectural
modernism of the IFC, but the mixture works perfectly. Prices are very
keen, especially in the evening when the menu opens out — Chicken
Jambalay, Fusilli with Courgettes and Mussels, dry baked Salmon with
Roasted Pepper and a Balsamic Vinaigrette. But it is at lunchtime, when
light pours in through the roof windows, through the sun-comprehending
glass, and you sit high on the balcony, that the IFC is best revealed for the
lovely space it is. Rumour has it they also show movies and that the seats
are comfy, but we have yet to manage to make it into the dark.

Open 12.30pm-11pm Mon-Sun
Closed Xmas
Average Price: bar snacks £2.50-£6, lunch £2-£4, restaurant £3-£8
Credit Cards: Visa, Access
No Service Charge (except 10% on parties of 6 or more)
Full Bar Licence
Wheelchair Access to bar (wheelchair friendly toilet)
Children — welcome
Recommended for Vegetarians
The IFC is next to Quaker House, just off Dame St.

KAPRIOL RESTAURANT

45 Camden Street Lwr, Dublin 2 Tel: (01) 475 1235 (298 5496 home)
Egidia and Giuseppe Peruzzi

It tends to be Italian restaurants which are the ones we most want to be friendly, unfussy, enduring little Mom'n'Pop sort of places. Places where they know your name, where you go late on a Friday, or early on a Tuesday to salve some domestic bruising, or where you select as your first choice to celebrate a good punt at the races, an exam scraped through, a job secured.

Egidia and Giuseppe Peruzzi's Kapriol is that place. Most of the customers are so well known to the Peruzzis that they almost order their food in pidgin Italian, that is if they do bother to order food, and don't just let Egidia see what she can come up with which will take their fancy. A fire will be lit in the grate, the seats are like little cubicles wrapped around with wood, and the interior design was in fashion sometime in the middle of the century, though that may not necessarily have been this century.

Egidia cooks the way she has always cooked: risotto alla veneziana, fettucine doppio burro, scallopine alla marsala o limone, chicken involtini, a timeless series of tunes and symphonies of flavour. Giuseppe, meanwhile, looks after the wines and the front of house, and to surrender to his judgement when it comes to something to drink is wisdom itself. The Kapriol is not to everyone's taste — often, one suspects, this lies with the fact that this is an expensive place, where many people believe that Italian food should always be cheap — but here you are paying for individuality, individual attention and individual cooking, the true characteristics of a Mom'n'Pop place, someplace to heal and to celebrate.

Open7.30pm-midnight (last orders) Mon-Sat
Closed bank holidays and 2 weeks in Aug
Average Price: dinner £20-£25
Credit Cards: Visa, Access/Master, Amex, Diners
12.5% Service Charge
Wine Licence
Wheelchair Access (but not to toilets)
Children — welcome
Varied Vegetarian dishes served each evening
At the southern end of Camden Street, on the corner where the road divides.

LA STAMPA

35 Dawson Street, Dublin 2 Tel: (01) 677 8611/677 3336
Louis Murray

Louis Murray has continued with his policy of attracting top-notch chefs to cook in La Stampa, following the run-away success which Michael Martin, formerly of Le Gavroche, enjoyed when he cooked here.

Mr Martin's successor is Paul Flynn, right-hand man to the tempestuous Nico Ladenis in his various London restaurants for a decade, and a cook of copious ability who enjoys working with the modish foods of the '90s whilst simultaneously dragging Irish standards up to date.

There is still some improving to be done with dishes such as ham and colcannon and his other native revisions, and Mr Flynn is at his best with fish cookery and in the splendid choice of sticky puddings. The dining room is perhaps the nicest in the entire country, and staff, curiously, can be both excellent and strangely lackadaisical. Prices are very keen.

Open 6.30pm-11pm Mon-Sat, noon-2pm Sun
Open all year incl Xmas day lunch
Average Price: lunch £12.50, dinner £9-£14
Credit Cards: Visa, Access/Master, Amex, Diners
No Service Charge (except 10% for parties of 6 and over)
Restaurant Licence
No Wheelchair Access
Children — no facilities
Vegetarian options always available
Opposite the Mansion House.

101 TALBOT

101-102 Talbot Street, Dublin 2 Tel: (01) 8745011
Margaret Duffy and Pascal Bradley

Margaret Duffy and Pascal Bradley's 101 Talbot has quietly
manoeuvered itself into a position where it is not just one of the best
restaurants in the capital, and not just one of the most admired, but
easily one of the most enjoyed. Everything this astute and amusing
pair do is devoted to making their restaurant work as a special space
in which to enjoy good food, good wine, good times. Walk up the stairs
from the dedicated grot of Talbot Street and this cocoon of good taste,
cool vibes, funky sounds and sweet service sets your soul at ease.
You can cast your mind back over many meals eaten here during the
last few years — lunches with mile-a-minute gossip amongst your
mates, quiet solo mid-afternoons with just some pasta and the
newspaper to peruse, happy dinners where bottle after bottle of Fetzer
Fumé Blanc or Wolfie Blass's Cab Sauv is resolutely demolished in the
cause of good cheer — and what is consistent is just how much the
charm, the atmosphere, the youthfulness and the bonhomie of 101
contribute to the cause of enjoying lunch or dinner.
Margaret Duffy's food is so enjoyably friendly that you will likely find
yourself day-dreaming about that parsnip soup, that brioche of
vegetables with a blue cheese dressing, that chicken stuffed with olives,
sun-dried tomatoes and mozzarella, that pecan pie or those oranges in
caramel and Cointreau. Ms Duffy's food always tastes like something
which she has, firstly, enjoyed cooking and, secondly, something she
would like to eat herself. This offering of personality through the food
and service of the restaurant is what makes 101 so special: without
Margaret and Pascal it would be nothing. Thanks to them, and their
unpretentiousness and calm, it is invaluable.

Open 10am-3pm Mon, 10am-11pm Tue-Sat (lunch served noon-3pm, dinner served
6.30pm-11pm)
Closed Xmas and bank holidays
Average Price: lunch £5-£10, dinner £12-£15
Credit Cards: Visa, Access/Master, Amex
No Service Charge (except for parties of over 8 persons)
Full Bar Licence
No Wheelchair Access
Children — high chairs
Recommended for Vegetarians
Talbot Street runs parallel to Abbey Street, and 101 is minutes from the Abbey
Theatre.

PIGALLE

14 Temple Bar, Merchant's Arch, Dublin 2 Tel: (01) 671 9262
Lahcen Iouani

Pigalle is aptly named, accurately suggesting Montmartre more than
Montparnasse, for this is a loose-limbed restaurant where the food
adds a dash of North Africa to a kitchen that is rooted in Paris. Like a
true French restaurant, Pigalle doesn't evolve or innovate much. It
simply does what it does — smooth puréed soups, rare lamb and beef
on well constructed sauces, gravity-defying pastries on colourful fruit
purées and fine vanilla custards — and does it with unmatched charm.
A rigorous culinary discipline lies behind a façade where the plates
don't match, the chairs and tables are bargain basement, where service
is sharply informal and the atmosphere is rather more retrograde right
bank than self-conscious left bank.

Open 12.30pm-3pm Mon-Fri, 7pm-10.30pm Mon-Sat
Closed Xmas and bank holidays
Average Price: lunch £11.50, dinner £18.50
Credit Cards: Visa, Access/Master
10% Service Charge
Wine Licence
No Wheelchair Access
Children — no facilities
Vegetarian dishes available on request
Pigalle is in the heart of the Temple Bar, on the first floor over Merchant's Arch.

THE RAJDOOT

26-28 Clarendon Street, Westbury Centre, Dublin 2 Tel: (01) 679 4274
Amarjit Gill

The Rajdoot offers not just the best Indian cooking in the city of
Dublin, but the finest and most alluring Indian cooking in the country.
Part of a small smart chain of Indian restaurants based in the U.K., the
Dublin outpost has distinguished itself by an impressive consistency
that has made it consistently interesting.

Part of a chain it may be, but the little bar at the entrance, with its
leather camel stools and embroidered brass bowls of torchy nuts,
chase away any feeling of factory-line production. The food echoes
this lushness in its stylish, instinctive, reverberant Moghul meld of
almonds, yogurt, spices and butter. Chicken Tikka is an institution of
Northern Indian food, Tandoori Mackerel or Tandoori Quail are more
unusual. Yet, with both, the restaurant succeeds in feathering the
suprisingly subtle tastes of a spicy marinade with the charcoal smoke
from the tandoor oven. The biryanis sufuse rice with the perfume of
cloves, whilst the fried sundries, the bhajees, the parathas are crisply
reviving in their salty oiliness.

Breads are more than marvellous, forming an integral part of the meal
should you abandon utensils and choose to use your fingers. Happily,
vegetarians are almost spoilt for choice. The service is formal and the
prices keen.

Open noon-2.30pm, 6.30pm-11.30pm Mon-Sat
Closed Xmas, New Year's Day, Good Fri (limited opening bank holidays)
Average Price: lunch £10, dinner £15
Credit Cards: Visa, Access/Master, Amex, Diners
12.5% Service Charge
Wine Licence
Wheelchair Access (happy to help negotiate steps, but no access to toilets)
Children — welcome
Recommended for Vegetarians
At the back of the Westbury Hotel.

RED BANK RESTAURANT

7 Church Street, Skerries, Co Dublin Tel: (01) 849 1005
Fax: (01) 849 1598
Terry McCoy

The way Terry McCoy does it, being chef and patron of a restaurant seems a piece of cake.

Source your foods from local growers, local suppliers, local fishmongers and fish smokers. Get your oysters from Carlingford Lough, conveniently just up the road, and flour from local flour grinders. You do this in order that the foods of the region will have the tastes of the region, and what you do, then, is to complete the equation, and cook them in the region.

Establish, then, your menu, and gently introduce the occasional innovation that has come from a trip abroad where you learnt of some alliance or some suitable technique which you find can be made to work in your own kitchen.

Cook, then, with grace and good humour, and get things right: smoked salmon with tarragon, steamed cockles and oysters, hake with the energetic kick of horseradish, perhaps a smoked loin of pork or roasted Barbary duck. The meat dishes in The Red Bank, like everything else, will be correct and flavourful, but it is with fish and shellfish that Mr McCoy shines, and you find yourself going 'ooh' and 'aah' with pleasure at the succulence and promise of each mouthful.

McCoy's object, as he himself will say, is to treat the foods with 'sympathy and respect', but he also knows that fish cookery is all about sources — local sources — and sauces, and he knows this better than almost anyone.

Open 7pm-10pm Tue-Sat, 12.30pm-2.15pm Sun
Closed Xmas
Average Price: dinner £17.95-£21
Credit Cards: Visa, Access/Master, Amex, Diners
No Service Charge
Restaurant Licence
Wheelchair Access
Children — controlled children welcome
Vegetarian options always available
Skerries is 29km north of Dublin and signposted from the N1 Dublin/Belfast road. The restaurant is in the centre of town.

ROLY'S BISTRO

7 Ballsbridge Terrace, Dublin 4 Tel: (01) 668 2611
Roly Saul

Roly Saul's eponymous venture has proven to be the biggest hit in Dublin's restaurant culture in recent times, and the clever anticipation and orchestration which underscores this restaurant reveals the shift in eating styles which is coursing through the restaurant trade.

For a start, though it is called a bistro this is really a brasserie — the upstairs dining room is handsome and endearing — but the prices belong almost to a café: lunch, in particular, is a whacking great bargain. Secondly, the food betrays no tension between culinary care and the necessary speed of service. The cooking is well crafted: poached cod, coq au vin, loin of pork, venison pie, all of it bistro fare that is suitable for lunch, perfect for dinner, food which suits pocket and paunch.

Finally, it is a fun place. No matter whether you are eight or eighty, the secret of Roly's success is that you can extract from it what you want: a quick lunch or a lingering dinner, a family party, maybe impressing the kids at the weekend when you have access and they don't want to go to the zoo again. Other restaurants in Dublin cottoned on to this idea of democracy and customer choice a while back, and they have likewise proven to be successes. Roly's is the latest addition to a pantheon where the demands of the punter are paramount. Its modest but hard-headed efficiency means that it deserves its success.

Open 12.30pm-3pm, 6pm-10pm Mon-Sun
Closed 24-27 Dec and Good Fri
Average Price: lunch £9.50, dinner £15-£19
Credit Cards: Visa, Access/Master, Amex
10% Service Charge
Restaurant Licence
Wheelchair Access
Children — no special facilities
Vegetarian options always available
On the corner between Ballsbridge and Herbert Park, just down from the American Embassy.

THE TEA ROOMS
Clarence Hotel, Dublin 7 Tel: (01) 677 6178 Fax: 677 7487
Michael Martin

You could call it post-modern irony, if you were a post-modern ironist, but there is something deliciously amusing in the fact that the hippest place to eat in Dublin is currently the restaurant in an ancient hotel which for years was a by-word for De Valerian Ireland.

The Clarence was the hotel where parish priests and parish-pump politicians stayed when they came to town. It was somewhere you could safely bring your grandparents to lunch, because you knew that they would get cabbage the way they liked it — boiled for 90 minutes with baking powder stirred into the cooking water — and beef the way they liked it — cooked to emaciated oblivion.

And now, just look at this. With Michael Martin in the kitchen and the copious coffers of U2 and Harry Crosbie to fund renovations, the Clarence Hotel and the Tea Rooms are, suddenly, a cool, happening space, so contemporary they are almost ahead of themselves, so post-modern it's almost a joke.

But Mr Martin's food is never a joke, thankfully. He resurrected the food in La Stampa before decamping across town, and the same stylishness and contemporary culinary obsessions are at play here: designer purple potatoes with a ragout of marinated chicken; slinky threads of saffron in a fine celeriac soup; a risotto of shellfish with, again, masses of saffron but, perhaps, a little too much shellfish stock; a deconstructed daube of beef with fine dumplings.

Deconstruction. Post-modernism. Irony. It may sound like an abstract impressionist's calling card, but Mr Martin's impression is far from abstract: this is food with good flavours and the smart dining room with its cool banquettes is distinctly — if we may borrow an adjective one would never, but never, have used of the old Clarence Hotel — groovy. The wine list still needs some work, staff are t-shirted but efficient, and the Tea Rooms seems doomed to success.

Open 10am-11.30am, 3pm-5.30pm Mon-Sat, noon-2.30pm (lunch), 6pm-11pm
(dinner) Mon-Sun
Closed Xmas
Average Price: table d'hôte £9.50-£12.50, à la carte £18-£22
Credit Cards: Visa, Access/Master, Amex, Diners
No Service Charge
Restaurant Licence
No Wheelchair Access
Children — welcome
Vegetarian options always available
The Clarence overlooks the river Liffey, from the south side.

ZEN CHINESE RESTAURANT

89 Upper Rathmines Road, Dublin 6 Tel: (01) 979428
Mr O'Conner

The Zen looks like a Chinese restaurant designed by a sinophile
Christian Missionary who wants to simultaneously praise the Lord,
practice with his chopsticks and, perhaps, repair his motorcycle. High-
beamed, the tables set wide apart, plain of ornamentation, it is church
hall meets college common room. It is, in fact, an old meeting hall, and
the feeling of spaciousness and light are a delightful antidote to the
over-heated design of all the other Chinese restaurants in town.
But, you can't eat furnishings, so it is a happy thing that the food is so
good, leaning mainly in the direction of Sichuan specialities: beef with
preserved vegetables on a bed of beansprouts is busy with the sharp
taste of peppercorns and black beans, whilst tofu adds a nicely soulish
taste. Dan Dan noodles are excellent, arriving in a deep, dark soup with
shoots of spring onion here and there. It is reassuring to see, also, a
modest sized menu rather than a huge array of dishes built around a
series of basic ingredients, and to encounter such subtle, real tastes.
The Zen is a nice surprise.

Open 12.30pm-2.30pm Thur, Fri & Sun, 6pm-midnight Mon-Sun
Closed Xmas
Average Price: lunch £8, dinner £22.50
Credit Cards: Visa, Access/Master, Amex, Diners
10% Service Charge
Wine Licence
Wheelchair Access
Children — welcome
Vegetarian food always available
At the 'Y' junction in Rathmines, take the left turn towards Upper Rathmines and the
restaurant is 300 yards up the street on the right hand side.

DESTRY RIDES AGAIN ➥ £

The Square, Clifden, Connemara, Co Galway Tel: (095) 21722
Patrick & Julia Foyle

It was Lord Beaverbrook who said that the sight of Marlene Dietrich
standing on a bar, in black net stockings, belting out 'See What The Boys
In The Back Room Will Have', was a greater work of art than the Venus
de Milo. Who would ever have believed that the noble lord would be such
an astute art critic, such an appreciator of the fine things in life? And who
of us would dare to disagree with his assessment?

Paddy Foyle's admiration of Marlene has extended not just to borrowing
the title from the classic western in which she starred with James Stewart,
but also some of the lady's capacity for re-invention. A desire to simplify
his food and to work in a funkier ambience has led to this splendid place
and with a talented young chef in Dermot Gannon, Destry gallops along
on good humour, good food and adrenalinated energy.

The cooking enjoys Mr Foyle's signature, that intuitive grasp for
motivating flavour in a dish and finding unusual alliances. The
marinated leg of lamb may seem as untypical an Irish dish as you
could imagine, the cubes of meat char-grilled to a rich spiciness and
offset by a chutney sauce, but the flavours could be found nowhere else
than the west coast. With a Barbary duck, Mr Foyle extracts the full
complement of rich flavours, whilst his fish cooking has always proved
to be feistily inventive, with clever experiments such as coating white
hake in black sesame seeds to produce a dish that dazzles both vision
and appetite.

Clifden has needed a place like Destry for a long time, somewhere that
matches the exuberance of the holidaymaker, somewhere kids just
adore, somewhere that pulses with the pleasure of good food and good
times. Just imagine if it was called The Venus De Milo. No, just can't
imagine it being called The Venus De Milo.

Open noon-10pm Mon-Sun
Closed Xmas and January
Average Price: lunch £5.50, dinner from £12.50
Credit Cards: Visa, Access/Master
No Service Charge
Wine Licence
Wheelchair Access
Children — always welcome, menus by arrangement
Vegetarian Option served each evening
Directions "Chiften town centre".

DRIMCONG HOUSE ★ £

Moycullen, Co Galway Tel: (091) 85115
Gerry & Marie Galvin

'My motivation and my guiding light is to experiment and, being Irish, to try to build on what we have', writes Gerry Galvin in his marvellous book of recipes, recollections and poems, 'The Drimcong Food Affair'. Mr Galvin, happily, is a man of action as much as a man of words, and if he is one of the leading intellects and thinkers in the world of Irish food, he is also one of its principal practical exponents.

His experiments are clever, creative and on-going, with each weekly menu drawing new ideas from the chef himself and his team, for Drimcong has begun over the years to establish itself as a superb training ground for young cooks, with a plenitude of youngsters emerging from under Mr Galvin's wings to carry off cooking awards and to begin to establish themselves as serious individuals.

His dish of black pudding and oysters with an apple and onion confit is already a legend, and he will improvise it into a marvellous black pudding mousse. This touch with rustic, obvious foods, this attempt to heighten and isolate flavours, is found in the Connemara lamb with a mousse of peas and a garlic gravy, in pigeon with couscous and a red wine sauce, a rabbit and venison pie with a chocolate flavoured sauce, in simple things such as colcannon soup, tipsy pudding, roast pike. There are marvellous foods for vegetarians — herb and parmesan omelette, polenta and aubergine gâteau — and for children — panfried chicken or grilled fish, ice-creams. Whatever one chooses, certain truths emerge about the cooking: it is deeply considered, and very generous in spirit, motivated by a hungry creativity, and it is distinctly Irish. Drimcong House, with its splendid staff and their obvious happiness and pride in their work, its sense of serenity and its respect for the efforts of those who work here and those who eat here, is a magnificent creation.

Open 7pm-9pm Tue-Sat
Closed Xmas-9 Mar
Average Price: dinner £14.95-£17.95
Credit Cards: Visa, Access/Master, Amex, Diners
10% Service Charge
Full Licence
Wheelchair Access (apart from three negotiable steps to hall)
Children — high chairs, children's menu £8.50
Recommended for Vegetarians
Drive out of Moycullen, towards Maam Cross, the restaurant is on your right.

ERRISEASK HOUSE HOTEL & RESTAURANT ➡

Ballyconneely, Clifden, Co Galway Tel: (095) 23553 Fax: 23639
Christian & Stefan Matz

Stefan Matz has the sort of culinary skills that other chefs would kill for. Indeed, Mr Matz has such a surfeit of skills and such a level of control, it might almost prove to be dangerous, and you fear that his ability to do anything anyway anytime anyhow might lead to food that was a marvel to look at and a triumph of pyrotechnical invention, but intended more for admiration and contemplation than degustation. Fear not. His fluency with classic techniques allows him to crossover culinary boundaries — a pot au feu of the sea, for example, a savarin of wild salmon, the teasing variation of magret of duck on a bed of homemade noodles — but his keenness for flavour never deserts him: a carpaccio of scallops, sliced terrifyingly thin, enjoys a beautiful directness of saline tastes, whilst his homemade noodles in a cream sauce of wild mushrooms trades the scent of the sea for the scent of woodland. A steamed fillet of turbot is served with salmon roe, the pink globules a salty antidote to the mellifluous fish, whilst this fondness for using a salty texture crops up in the Connemara lamb, the loin boned and a perfect gratinate of fine herbs cutting the sweet meat.

The dishes, of course, look magnificent, right from a little amusée through to rich, colourful desserts. This alliance of appearance and appetite makes his food quite thrilling, and with a good bottle of German wine — the Schloss Johannisberg Reisling Kabinett, from an estate in the Rheingau which restricts its yields to 55-65 hectolitres per hectare, is one of the greatest arguments for the nobility of the Reisling grape which you can find in Ireland — you can have a dynamic dinner. The atmosphere, however, should try to find an extra trace of lightheartedness, for whilst this is serious cooking, it is not po-faced: it is here to be enjoyed.

Open 6.30pm-9.30pm Mon-Sun
Closed 1 Nov-1 Apr
Average Price: dinner £21.50-£29
Credit Cards: Visa, Access/Master, Amex, Diners
No Service Charge
Restaurant Licence
No Wheelchair Access
Children — high chairs
Vegetarian menus by arrangement
Take the coast road from Clifden to Ballyconneely, then follow the signposts.

HIGH MOORS RESTAURANT

Dooneen, Clifden, Co Galway Tel: (095) 21342
Hugh & Eileen Griffin

There are certain places, certain restaurants, which are just the sort
of place you dream of discovering when you are on holiday.
You would like to find someplace where the food had something of a
domestic character, indeed where the restaurant itself had a domestic
character; almost as if someone was welcoming you into their home.
And you would hope that the food would be simply cooked, quietly
expressive of its own tastes and flavours. And you would hope the
service would be serene and calm, for you want, really, a night which
begins slowly but then, gradually, takes off, until soon it is sometime in
the small hours and that voice you are hearing in that pub singing that
song is...well, your voice, actually.
High Moors is the place to kick off an evening like this, a holiday special.
It opens at Easter, closes in the autumn, and in between Hugh and Eileen
Griffin welcome people into a restaurant which is, in fact, their home.
You can look out across the wild, remorseless moors as sunset falls, and
await the quiet pleasures of Eileen Griffin's food. It will be simple food
but it will taste delicious because a lot of it will have been grown by Hugh
himself, just a stone's throw down the road. The rest will have been
sourced locally, and Eileen knows how to get the best out of it. Brill will
have a red pepper and chive sauce, duck breast a purée of apple, sage
and onion. With some of their own gravadlax to begin and maybe some
summer berries and currants in brandy syrup for dessert, you will smile
and say that you have found that place you were thinking of. And, then,
off to the pub, and that song that beats in your head.

Open 7pm-9.30pm Wed-Sun
Closed Nov-Apr
Average Price: dinner £12
Credit Cards: Visa, Access/Master
10% Service Charge
Wine Licence
Wheelchair Access
Children — high chairs and half portions
Varied Vegetarian Menu served each evening
Look for the sign 1km from Clifden directing you to a side road off the main
Ballyconneely road.

MAINISTIR HOUSE HOSTEL £

Inis Mór, Aran Islands, Co Galway Tel: (099) 61169 Fax: 61351
Joël d'Anjou, Tara Rafferty and Mairtin Mullen

Eating in Mainistir, like staying in Mainistir, throws up a series of
surprises, banishes all pre-conceptions, here in a hostel where you can
sit in leather armchairs reading copies of Gramophone or GQ, a place
with a restaurant where the favoured seats are, actually, in the kitchen.
It works through the vision of Joël d'Anjou with the circle completed
by Tara Rafferty and Mairtin Mullen. M d'Anjou makes it work by
being a cultured man without a trace of snobbery, by being a private
person who loves to share his space with people. Tara Rafferty gives
the place a sense of energy and organisation and Mairtin Mullen brings
the necessary humour to it all in both his tours of the island and his
quiet presence in the hostel.
Each evening, after a countdown worthy of NASA, hostellers, guests and
non-resident visitors pile into a 'Vaguely Vegetarian' buffet: great North
African platters weighted with pulses and salads, gifted with swirls of
pasta threaded through snippets of smoked salmon, laced with cream,
neat triangles of crab quiche or untidy slabs of pepper pizza.
It is sublime food, offered at a knockdown price and presented in an
atmosphere that, at times, can seem to be the essence of Aranness:
sociable, intelligent, on the edge, apart, an idea made real.

Open for dinner 8pm sharp (7.30pm winter)
Open all year incl Xmas
Average Price: dinner £6
Credit Cards: Visa, Access/Master
No Service Charge
No Licence (bring your own)
No Wheelchair Access
Children — welcome
Recommended for Vegetarians
When you arrive on the pier or the airport ask for Mairtin.

O'GRADY'S SEAFOOD RESTAURANT
Market Street, Clifden, Co Galway Tel: (095) 21450
The O'Grady family

For many visitors to the bracingly boisterous resort town of Clifden,
O'Grady's Seafood Restaurant is as automatic a stop as St. Peter's in
Rome or Mulligan's bar in Dublin. The food the O'Grady family serve,
an easeful essay on good flavours and simple ingredients, explains the
restaurant's enduring success, right from first bite to last.
Everything here is designed to make the diner feel comfortable, and to
usher in a relaxed time. The lighting is low, the tables are intimately
arranged if you want, socially arranged if you don't, service is
charming, and the fillets of fish are fresh, the cuts of meat are
flavourful, the bread is good, the desserts are sinfully sweet. The
business of the O'Grady family has always been to look after people,
and they do that by doing their best to help you have a good time,
whether you want a simple family lunch, a single plate of food, or a
grander dinner to mark the end of a happy holiday.

Open noon-2.30pm, 7pm-10pm Tue-Sat
Closed Dec-Mar (open Xmas and New Year)
Average Price: lunch £9, dinner £18
Credit Cards: Visa, Access/Master, Amex
No Service Charge
Full Licence
Wheelchair Access to restaurant but not to toilets
Children — over 5yrs welcome
Vegetarian options always available
In the centre of Clifden.

ROYAL VILLA

13 Shop Street, Galway, Co Galway Tel: (091) 63450 Fax: 68828
Charles Chan

Galway is one of the nicest cities in Ireland.

Indeed it may well be the nicest.

It is certainly the most festive, enjoys the best market you will find
anywhere on the island, and the countryside around it is blessed with
the presence of growers and food producers whose standards are
unerringly high. Galway's pubs are brilliant.

It is on the coast, so there is plenty of fresh fish and shellfish, and
western breezes should ensure the finest beef and lamb.

Why, then, does Galway not enjoy an embarrassment of fine
restaurants?

It attracts zillions of tourists and has a rich cultural life right throughout
the year, yet its eating houses seem unable to match the standards of
those places which are not too distant: the excellent oyster bars south
of the city, the fine restaurants of north County Clare, the dedicated
individuals such as Gerry Galvin who cook west of the city as you head
towards Connemara. Galway has everything, and it has a great deal of
food and places to eat, but it has no cooks who work at the cutting edge,
no celebrated individuals whose inventions and improvisations have
earned them welcome reputations. This is an inexplicable fact, and one
which some bright spark will, soon, exploit to the full.

So, let us give thanks, then, for Charles Chan and the high standards
he maintains in the Royal Villa, smack in the centre of the city. His
Chinese food has always been good, his standards have always been
high and, thereby, he has revealed the weaknesses of other restaurants
in Galway city.

Open 12.30pm-2.30pm Mon-Fri, 6pm-midnight Mon-Thur, 6pm-12.30am Fri-Sat, 1pm-
midnight Sun
Closed 25-26 Dec
Average Price: lunch £5-£10, dinner £16
Credit Cards: Visa, Access/Master, Amex, Diners
10% Service Charge
Wine Licence
No Wheelchair Access
Children — high chairs and menu prices from £5
Recommended for Vegetarians
Galway city centre.

BEGINISH RESTAURANT

Green Street, Dingle, Co Kerry Tel: (066) 51588
John & Pat Moore

Pat Moore is a serious cook, and a seriously skilful one. She has already created one of the most talked-about dishes in recent years in Ireland with her hot rhubarb soufflé tart, a dish of such ethereal tenderness and drop-dead deliciousness that it hits the senses with the shock of waking from a dream. But there is much more to her skills than those of the talented patissier.

Her cooking has the hallmarks of a cook who is hungrily inquisitive, her dishes are full of those little gestures which announce the improvisations and experimentations of a cook who wants to learn more and more. One of the greatest errors made by many chefs is their disinterest in the work of their peers. Mrs Moore has not only eaten the food of the great chefs, she is a perceptive critic of the work of even the most luminary individuals, and she knows how to assimilate the strengths of other people's work into her cooking, and how to avoid their shortcomings.

Where this comes most happily into play is in her appreciation for flavour, and the need to locate and capture the integral flavour of an ingredient whilst contrasting or comforting it with an apposite sauce. With flaky, sweet crab meat, she will combine the shellfish with a chive mayonnaise, whilst tender pinky prawns will have a sharply spiced mayonnaise to play against. A fillet of turbot will sit on a scrumptious bed of potato purée with a clean chive sauce circling the dish, whilst roasted john dory will have a dazzlingly colourful brunoise of vegetables tapestried around the dish with a creamy mustard sauce perfectly accenting the freshness and liveliness of the fish. Tastes are very positive and happy, and the sense of balance in the main courses is instinctively judged.

The wine list is excellent, the service perfect, the ambience utterly apposite. When in Dingle, you want to be in Beginish, simple as that.

Open 12.30pm-2.15pm, 6pm-9.30pm Tue-Sun
Closed mid Nov-mid Mar
Average Price: lunch £7, dinner £17
Credit Cards: Visa, Access/Master, Amex, Diners
No Service Charge
Full Pub Licence
No Wheelchair Access
Children — welcome
Varied Vegetarian dishes served each evening
Almost opposite the Catholic church, half way up Green Street at the top of the town.

D'ARCY'S OLD BANK HOUSE

Main Street, Kenmare, Co Kerry Tel & Fax: (064) 41589
Matthew and Aileen d'Arcy

Matt d'Arcy's Old Bank House may be set in somewhat simpler
premises than the grandeur of The Park Hotel, his old stomping
ground just down the hill in Kenmare, where he was head chef for
many years, but the rich complexity and lavish culinary control of
d'Arcy's cooking are every bit as evident here as before.

His love of variation and complication runs wild throughout a long and
agonising-to-choose-from menu: a warm ravioli of prawn mousse with
a sweet pepper scented butter, mussel tartlet, salmon with noodles in a
light curry sauce, chicken and noodle soup with star anise, scallops
fried in the pan with leeks and grapes, a chilled orange soufflé. One is
always struck by the fact that this cooking, with its impressive
architecture of design and concentrated focus of taste, is very classic
and, at the same time, very modern. The dining room is simple, best on
cool evenings with the fire bright, and a good bottle to enjoy with this
good food.

Open 5pm-10.30pm Mon-Sun (Apr-Oct), 7pm-10.30pm Fri-Sun (Oct-Mar)
Closed Xmas
Average Price: dinner £15-£20
Credit Cards: Visa, Access/Master, Diners
No Service Charge
Wine Licence
Wheelchair Access
Children — welcome, half portions
Vegetarian options only available on request
At the top end of Main Street.

GABY'S

17 High Street, Killarney, Co Kerry Tel: (064) 32519
Geert & Marie Maes

Gaby's has moved a little bit further up the street from its old location in Killarney but its signature sign of an upturned corrach with three male figures underneath transporting the boat along a shore means it is easily discoverable. The signature sign has stayed the same and so has the consistency and effectiveness of Geert Maes' cooking. In a town full of froth and flotsam and endless menus packed with ersatz food, Mr Maes is a serious cook, and Gaby's is just the sort of restaurant you desperately want to find in Killarney, especially on one of those days when the streets are clogged with human traffic and you clamour for respite.

The restaurant is almost a café in style, with the cooking concentrating on Mr Maes' strength with fish and shellfish: a shellfish platter, black sole in a cream sauce, hot salmon or hot smoked trout, their own secret way of preparing lobster fresh from the tank, just right for an informal lunch, and a romantic dinner.

Open 12.30pm-2.30pm Tue-Sat, 6pm-10pm Mon-Sat
Closed Xmas week and Feb
Average Price: lunch £2.95-£6, dinner £10-£26
Credit Cards: Visa, Access/Master, Amex, Diners
10% Service Charge
Restaurant Licence
Wheelchair Access
Children — high chairs and half portions
Vegetarian meals with prior notice
Killarney Town Centre.

LOAVES & FISHES

Caherdaniel, Co Kerry Tel: (0667) 5273
Helen Mullane & Armel White

They are a good twosome, Helen Mullane and her man Armel White.
Together, they deliver a splendid confection in Loaves and Fishes,
making this one of those places which you dream about finding when
you are travelling or touring or just plain loafing around.
She sets the tone at front of this intimate house at just that right
combination of bashful holiday happiness — candlelit tables,
comforting crooners on the stereo — while he takes care of the culinary
ambience — the busy sounds of whisking, slicing and sizzling coming
from the kitchen reassure as to the trueness of the restaurant, and the
aromas of something brewing or reducing drift out to the dining room
and set the appetite up for the evening.
Mr White's food trades on deep flavours and his aim is to find a new
fusion of tastes by means of unexpected combinations. So smoked
salmon will be grilled, and then have some warame scattered on top.
Quail's eggs may be poached in red wine, fresh prawns will be
scampied, and some roast duck will be sharply counterpointed by a
blackcurrant sauce. Whatever diversities he chooses, however, Mr
White proves himself able to make the dish work, and with some
simple but ruddy vegetables and fine, sticky desserts, you find this
food is extremely enjoyable and companionable. In the context of the
romantic, careless and carefree calm of the restaurant, it is just the
food you wanted. Prices are splendidly modest, and just another part
of this charming miracle.

Open 6pm-9.30pm Tue-Sun
Closed Oct-Easter (closed Tue in low season)
Average Price: dinner £18-£20
Credit Cards: Visa, Access
No Service Charge
Wine Licence
Wheelchair Access (but not to toilet)
Children — no facilities
No function rooms
Vegetarian dishes on request
Caherdaniel is on the Ring of Kerry about 45 mins from Kenmare.

NICK'S RESTAURANT

Lower Bridge Street, Killorglin, Co Kerry Tel: (066) 61219
Nicholas Foley

Crowds and crowds of carefree carousers flock to this cheerful pub-cum-restaurant in the hilly town of Killorglin, meaning that whether or not it is, in fact, an early Tuesday evening in the middle of a wet September, or maybe just a wet Wednesday sometime in early April, Nick's enjoys the celebratory atmosphere of a Friday night wedding. The food accentuates the festivity of the place, with bumper Saturday night specials like rack of lamb, fillets of fish in creamy sauces and simple, superb steaks from Kerry cattle, all launched at the punters in grand portions and with sweet charm. To begin the evening, several drinks in the bar, as you listen to the whooping choruses on the piano, is imperative before you even consider ordering anything to eat.

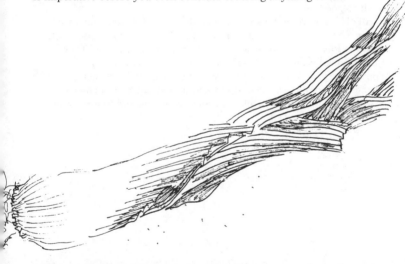

Open 12.30pm-2.30pm, 6pm-10pm Mon-Sun
Closed Xmas, Nov, lunch from Sept-Easter, Mon-Tue from Jan-Mar
Average Price: lunch & bar food £6-£10, dinner £18-£25
Credit Cards: Visa, Access/Master, Amex, Diners
No Service Charge
Full Bar Licence
Wheelchair Access to restaurant
Children — half portions
Vegetarian stir fry always available
Half way up the hill on the road coming from Tralee or Killarney.

PACKIE'S ➡ £

Henry Street, Kenmare, Co Kerry Tel: (064) 41508
Maura Foley

It was a desire to simplify her food and to cut prices which led Maura Foley to begin this smashing venture, and this wise foresight is typical of the same simple genius that you find in her cooking.

This is a happy, up-for-it place to eat, with great staff, great prices and a wonderful bistro buzz. Simple foods cooked in here seem almost a revelation, their taste is so real, so true. John Dory with a herb beurre blanc. Scallops with Noilly Prat and mushrooms, even time-abused classics like Sole meuniere or crab claws in garlic butter have stupendous, fresh, vigorous tastes, and that is before you get around to some spoonsome vanilla ice-cream which will beggar belief it is so fine. You name it, and you will scarcely be able to remember when you last ate it so good.

Mrs Foley is a brilliant cook, and a modest, ever-learning one, which is how she manages to keep ever-ahead of the posse who would try to filch her ideas and who always, but always, get them wrong. They get them wrong because they don't have Mrs Foley's patience or application, they don't have her sense of culinary balance, her gift for giving delight in a dish. The trip to Kenmare to eat Maura Foley's food is one of the most worthwhile, pleasure-promising and well-rewarded trips you can make.

Open 5.30pm-10pm Mon-Sat
Closed end Dec-end Feb
Average Price: dinner £12
Credit Cards: Visa, Access/Master
No Service Charge
Wine Licence
Wheelchair Access (through side door)
Children — welcome
Vegetarian options always available
In the centre of Kenmare.

THE PARK HOTEL

Kenmare, Co Kerry Tel: (064) 41200
Francis Brennan

If one were to hold a poll of hoteliers to find the hoteliers' hotelier, no one would lay a bet with you that the winner would not be Francis Brennan. Mr Brennan is, quite simply, the very personification, the very essence, of the hotelier. His skills are so effortless and so graceful that you can't imagine that he ever actually learnt them. Far more likely, you reckon, that he was born this way, popped from the womb with this integral and instinctive grasp of how to run an hotel to the very highest standards, and then some.

It is Francis Brennan who personifies and motivates The Park Hotel, articulates its thoughtfulness and appositeness, ensures that the food is correct, that the rooms are perfect, makes it the place it is, makes it like no other place. It is impossible, then, to divorce this fact from the enjoyment of a meal here. One will admire Brian Cleere's cooking for the harmony and well-tuned balance which he brings to his work and for the simplicity he has introduced to the menu — and the fact that it is now written in English — and one will enjoy fillet of beef with a chartreuse of oxtail, onion confit and a red wine glaze, or a terrine of guinea fowl and pigeon with warm vegetables and truffle vinaigrette, and the superb local fish and shellfish — but the food is just one part of a jigsaw involving the lovely dining room with its sweep-away views, and the brilliant service, and the grandness of the Park and its ability to avoid any sense of preciousness or snobbery.

Open 1pm-1.45pm, 7pm-8.45pm Mon-Sun
Closed 2 Jan-15 April and mid Nov-23rd Dec
Average Price: lunch £18, dinner £36
Credit Cards: Visa, Access/Master, Amex, Diners
No Service Charge
Full Pub Licence
Wheelchair Access
Children — high chairs, children's menu, £8
Vegetarian dishes only with prior notice
At the top of the slopes of the village of Kenmare, The Park is well signposted.

SHEEN FALLS LODGE
Kenmare, Co Kerry Tel: (064) 41600
Fergus Moore

Sheen Falls Lodge plights its troth, unambiguously, at high rolling, free-spending travellers, folk with a taste for restrained décor and lavish food. You might find yourself dining alongside visiting foreign royalty in the La Cascade Restaurant, find yourself in the presence of stars and their agents, pulp novelists with healthy current accounts. If you do, don't worry: whilst they will be certain to recognise you, they are unlikely to table-hop.

Fergus Moore's cooking is luxurious in design and execution. He will contemporise super-duper foods such as foie gras by means of the vogueish use of balsamic vinegar, or allying smoked duck breast with deep fried haricots. The ideal he pursues is that of a principal ingredient married to a sympathetic staple and a rich sauce, as in dishes such as duck with roasted garlic and Sloe gin essence, or turbot and john dory on braised leeks with a chive butter sauce. Desserts are equally lavish: hot chocolate soufflé with a pistachio and white chocolate ice-cream, Ceylon tea parfait with cinnamon biscuits and a lime caramel glaze.

Many will relish this unapologetically lush style of food, just as they will relish the hotel's unapologetically lush style of decoration and the svelte service and the dream-like character of the whole experience.

Open 7.30pm-9.30pm Mon-Sun
Closed early Jan-mid Mar
Average Price: dinner £35
Credit Cards: Visa, Access/Master, Amex, Diners
No Service Charge
Full Licence
Full Wheelchair Access
Children — menus £10-£15
Vegetarian menu always available
One kilometre outside Kenmare on the Glengarriff road.

THE STRAWBERRY TREE ➡

24 Plunkett Street, Killarney, Co Kerry Tel: (064) 32688
Evan Doyle

Evan Doyle has always been the most perspicacious of restaurant proprietors. He has always run the restaurants he has been associated with in pursuit of an ideal of good food rather than mere profit, always looking for ways in which to sharpen his focus as to how a restaurant should operate, what food a restaurant should serve in order to acquire its own personality, how he and his staff should work in order to ensure that customers have not just a good time, but a memorable experience. In The Strawberry Tree, his calm and quite lovely restaurant in the overheated and often-unlovely town of Killarney, Mr Doyle has taken a brave step into the future, by virtue of an insistence on sourcing all his foods from local, artisan and organic sources. The Strawberry Tree offers a taste of the future, and my goodness, but it sure tastes good. It tastes good by virtue of venison from that dazzlingly talented butcher Armin Weise from Fossa, because of the true taste of the organic vegetables from Jo Barth which are imported in from County Cork, a job Mr Doyle undertakes himself. There is free range beef from Thady Crowley, and free range duck and chicken from Barry's farm. Pat Spillane from just down the street and around the corner supplies fresh fish and shellfish, and everything, but everything, has the stamp and signature of its supplier on it: on the menu are the written guarantees from them all, their determination to supply the best and nothing but. 'Real Foods' is what they call it, and the results are truly sublime. Corned beef parcelled up in a pouch of cabbage with a parsley sauce inside, fillet of beef chocolate-rich and deep in flavour, meltingly elusive smoked salmon, herby, sweet mountain lamb. This ingenuity and foresight makes this charming, intimate restaurant even more valuable. The staff, incidentally, are amongst the very best in the country.

Open 6pm-10pm Tue-Sat (lunch on request — check all times out of season)
Closed Dec-Mar
Average Price: dinner £16
Credit Cards: Visa, Access/Master, Amex, Diners
10% Service Charge
Wine Licence
No Wheelchair Access
Children — high chairs
Vegetarian options always available
Killarney town centre.

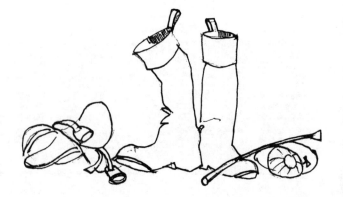

TONLEGEE HOUSE

Athy, Co Kildare Tel: (0507) 31473
Mark and Marjorie Molloy

'I should like particularly to congratulate the Molloys. Nothing was ever too much trouble, and the food was exceptional'. This remark in a letter from an English traveller who could declare that during their holiday in Ireland — with a couple of exceptions — 'everyone, everything and everywhere was magnificent', is the kind of talk-talk you hear about Mark and Marjorie Molloy's Tonlegee House.

Partly, this affection is built on the basis of Mark Molloy's cooking, an ambitious, charged cuisine which wraps itself up in culinary complexities — boudin of chicken with pistachio nuts and a Pommery mustard sauce, escalope of salmon with mussels and a fresh basil sauce, guinea fowl with roast garlic and a thyme flavoured jus, chocolate and almond flavoured marjolaine (this a dish in tribute to his wife, perhaps?) — but which is always capable of making flavours hit home, creating dishes that are often truly memorable.

But it is the atmosphere created by a young couple working hard in their own place and slowly improving it, slowly knocking it to rights, adding on a quintet of comfy rooms to truly turn it into a restaurant with rooms, it is this motivation which creates the energy and the thrill of Tonlegee, makes it a place where nothing is, indeed, too much trouble.

Open 7pm-9.30pm Mon-Thur, 7pm-10.30pm Fri-Sat
Closed Xmas
Average Price: dinner £20
Credit Cards: Visa, Access/Master
No Service Charge
Full Licence
No Wheelchair Access (though happy to help)
Children — no facilities
Vegetarian dishes always available (notice helps)
In Athy, cross two bridges and take the Kilkenny road out of town. Very soon you will see their sign telling you to go left.

LACKEN HOUSE ➡

Dublin Road, Kilkenny, Co Kilkenny Tel: (056) 61085 Fax: 62435
Eugene & Breda McSweeney

You could select any dish from the menus which Eugene McSweeney
prepares and cooks in Lacken House, the homely, peaceful restaurant
with rooms which he and his wife Breda run just on the outskirts of
Kilkenny, and no matter what the choice — steamed breast of chicken
with a nettle mousse, let's say, or goose with a purse of apple and
walnut stuffing, poached silver bream with tomato and fresh herb
sauce — and no matter what the individual tastes and the distinct
techniques which would be involved, you will find yourself always
confronted by two simple truths.

The first is that with everything he cooks, Mr McSweeney exploits the
long-learnt skill of the professional cook — the chicken will be perfect,
the goose hearty yet refined, the poached silver bream was described
by a writer for America's Bon Appetit as 'one of the best fish dishes I've
ever eaten'. Skill, here, is used to extract flavour, to reveal the character
and essence of a food. Mr McSweeney never shows off, never lets
things get complicated just for the hell of it.

But you will also find that the cooking shows someone who has never lost
touch with the scents, attractions and satisfactions of the garden and the
ground: he likes to spirit the green, wild tastes of herbs and leaves such
as nettles and parsley into dishes to offer a counterpoint to the luxury of
prime cuts and complex tastes. He keeps his chain of suppliers as short as
possible, though he will wander down as far south as Clonakilty to secure
Edward Twomey's black pudding in order to make his livelysome twice-
baked black pudding soufflé, but otherwise everything is local. Local, also,
is the character of Lacken House, the staff are warmly welcoming, and
you find the true tastes of Irish food, and Irish hospitality, here.

Open 7pm-10.30pm Tue-Sat
Closed Xmas Day
Average Price: dinner £22
Credit Cards: Visa, Access/Master, Amex, Diners
No Service Charge
Restaurant Licence
No Wheelchair Access
Children — high chair and special menu
Recommended for Vegetarians
On the Dublin Road just as you drive into Kilkenny from the north, just past the
roundabout.

THE MOTTE

Inistioge, Co Kilkenny Tel: (056) 58655
Alan Walton & Tom Reade-Duncan

As a restaurant, Alan Walton and Tom Reade-Duncan's The Motte
makes consummate sense. Its carefully confected contrivance makes
for a charmingly regressive space, creating just exactly how you want
a restaurant dining room to be when you are out for that special night,
just how you want a restaurant dining room to appear when you walk
in out of the evening.

Drapes tumble and flow to the ground and shudder up to the ceiling,
the art on the wall is striking, full of presence, the music is stagey
and whacky. Gleaming glasses gleam, linen is crisp and tactile. It is
a genuinely intimate little room, a small theatre for eating: five tables,
low lights, service which works at a properly pedestrian pace, slowing
you down and setting you up for the evening.

Alan and Tom like to tinker and toy with tastes, like to twist conventional
cooking slightly awry, so calf's liver comes sweet and sour, smoked salmon
has an orange couscous, a mango purée completes the Pacific Rim tour
which a coconut crêpe contributes to a warm breast of chicken.

Pork cooked in milk is nothing new, but pork fillet with coconut milk
is, while roasted pheasant has not only a deep chocolate sauce but
also a scattering of Chinese straw mushrooms to add an unexpected
savoury note to a cloying and rich dish.

It is all good fun, this playfulness with contrasts and confections,
though desserts opt simply for blow-me! deliciousness: sticky
profiteroles or a white chocolate cheesecake.

Alan and Tom orchestrate the controlled waywardness of The Motte
perfectly, with clever gags, digressions into local history, friendly chit-
chat. A charming evening, a charming restaurant, a charming village.
The name, incidentally, is not pronounced in the way a Dublin youth
might use the sound to describe his girlfriend — 'mott' — but takes
on a refined, Kilkenny character to become 'moat'.

Open 7pm-10pm Wed-Sun (open Tue Jun-Sept)
Closed Xmas and bank holidays
Average Price: dinner £18.50
Credit Cards: Visa, Access/Master, Amex
No Service Charge
Wine Licence
Wheelchair Access, but not to toilets
Children — no facilities
Vegetarian dinner available, given 24 hours notice
Just up the hill in Inistioge, in the centre of town.

THE MUSTARD SEED
Adare, Co Limerick Tel: (061) 396451
Daniel Mullane

There is a simple answer to the public relations and culinary problems of County Limerick.

Celebrated as somewhere unlikely to detain the traveller or the eater overlong, Limerick should — and tomorrow will not be a day too soon — appoint Mr Daniel Mullane as President and main man of the county. Mr Mullane will have carte blanche to improve the quality of life in this strangely bourgeois place.

His qualification for seizing the job is, simply, that he runs a restaurant — The Mustard Seed — which is not just one of the best in the country, but which, in its thoughtful, tasteful, considered, creative way of working, shows every other place in Limerick up for the joints they are. He will solve the matter of crime by using the same charm with which he suffuses his restaurant. He will attend to the matter of the county's less than picturesque towns and villages by designing them to look as much like Adare as possible, for Adare is heartbreakingly lovely. Any difficulty with bureaucrats, roads, water and so on will be solved by the efficiency which Mr Mullane and his chef, Michael Weir, attend to every business. Just look at the way, for example, Mr Weir invents a series of personal creations, specially for vegetarians, ranging from a mélange of roasted vegetables on a base of tomato tagliatelle with a roast pimento sauce, through to twice baked spinach and Gruyère soufflé with lasagne of garden vegetables on a tomato purée, striving to make his dishes 'full of flavour, colourful and interesting, as I feel too often that vegetarian dishes are dull and thrown together in the kitchen at the last minute and this should not be so'.

Could there be a greater electoral platform? We would have to insist, of course, that Mr Mullane's duties did not take him away from the Mustard Seed. Saving Limerick may be important, but it's not that important.

Open 7pm-10pm Tue-Sat
Closed Xmas
Average Price: dinner from £23
Credit Cards: Visa, Access/Master, Amex, Diners
No Fixed Service Charge
Restaurant Licence
Wheelchair Access to restaurant, but not to toilets
Children — no facilities
Recommended for Vegetarians
In the centre of Adare village.

ECHOES

Main Street, Cong, Co Mayo Tel: (092) 46059
Siobhan, Tom & Helen Ryan

When it comes to talking or singing about a family affair, Sly Stone would have to write an opera to unravel the parental and sibling set-up which accounts for the success of Echoes.

Whilst Siobhan Ryan garners most of the attention — quite right, of course, for she is the person who devises the dishes and is the instrumental force in getting them from stove to table — she could not do so without her Dad, who takes care of all manner of supplies to the restaurant, and young Tom, the brother, who is not only an award-winning butcher, but also not above hopping into the kitchen to rattle the pots and pans when Siobhan takes a deserved break.

Siobhan's sister brings to the job of waiting on table a feline grace and a skill which turns her work into an art form and, finally, Siobhan's mother, who welcomes you, organises the bills and cooks breakfast in the restaurant during the summer months, completes this extraordinary picture.

Together, the family all work to the benefit of the fine food you can expect in Echoes: home-smoked wild salmon on top of a springy bed of crisp salad leaves; breaded monkfish between slabs of green bacon and onions and peppers; fat scallops into a mornay sauce served on the shell surrounded by piped potato; sweet mountain lamb; ice-creams which are the stuff you scream for in your dreams.

This deeply comforting food, full of odoriferous scents and rich with goodness, comes in grandly generous portions, and the happy family affair of Echoes is as far removed from the self-conscious sense of denial that pervades Mayo as you could imagine.

Open 6pm-10pm Mon-Sun (shorter hours during winter season).
Open all year
Average Price: dinner £8-£14
Credit Cards: Visa, Access/Master, Amex
No Service Charge
Restaurant Licence
Wheelchair Access
Children — high chairs and special menus
Vegetarian options always available
Echoes is right in the centre of Cong, next to the butcher's.

DUNDERRY LODGE RESTAURANT

Dunderry, Robinstown, Co Meath Tel: (046) 31671
Paul Groves

In the midst of the agricultural cradle of County Meath, in an enviably obscure and out-of-the-way location and in an enviably dignified building which mixes hay barn with high style, Paul Groves cooks a very personal interpretation of hâute cuisine in the Dunderry Lodge Restaurant.

His orientation is decidedly modern, with modish borrowings from the fresh tastes of the Mediterranean — lamb served with a tomato and basil jus, a dressing of tapenade for a chicken and bacon terrine — and influences from both the Middle and Far East — beef with shiitake mushrooms, or on Chinese leaves with a five spice sauce. The cooking is clever, and enjoyable because the tastes are succinctly delivered, properly achieved and elegantly served, and everything enjoys Mr Groves' ability to reveal basic, integral tastes and to find harmonious accord between them.

Open 12.30pm-2.30pm, 7pm-9.30pm Tue-Sat
Closed Xmas and 1 week in Jan and Aug
Average Price: lunch £13.50, dinner £20
Credit Cards: Visa, Access/Master, Amex
No Service Charge
Restaurant Licence
No Wheelchair Access
Children — no facilities
Recommended for Vegetarians
From Navan take the Athboy road. Drive four-and-a-half miles and you will see the signs for Dunderry village and then Dunderry Lodge.

CROMLEACH LODGE

Ballindoon, Boyle, Co Sligo Tel: (071) 65155 Fax: 65455
Christy and Moira Tighe

Cromleach Lodge is a monument to painstaking application. Neither Christy nor Moira Tighe have a background in the business of running a restaurant with rooms, but their determination to improve, their will to succeed, has meant that Cromleach has steadily acquired an impressive reputation over the last years.

Moira Tighe's cooking exploits two central commands: firstly, she uses impeccable ingredients from local growers, the bulk of the vegetables and herbs being organically grown, and, secondly, despite being self-taught, her cooking strides confidently between modern improvisations — a sausage of chicken and crab, for example — and the classic verities where her work can seem most confidently at home: Lough Gill salmon on a bed of spinach with a lemon and saffron sauce with white wine, a goat's cheese salad sharply attenuated with vivacious fresh herbs, perfectly subtle and sweet roasted lamb, intricately fine desserts.

It is obvious that Mrs Tighe admires the work of Anton Mosimann, the love of colour and the implication that every plate is a canvas fit to be framed with food in a culinary picture. But, whilst worshipping at the shrine of such an individual cook can often be a slightly dangerous thing for an acolyte, for Mr Mosimann's signature is fiercely strong and individual, the food in Cromleach usually finds its own feet, and this is when it is truly at its best.

Open 7pm-9pm Mon-Sat, 6.30pm-8.30pm Sun
Closed 23 Dec-21 Jan
Average Price: dinner £26.50
Credit Cards: Visa, Access/Master, Amex, Diners
No Service Charge
Restaurant Licence
Wheelchair Access only with assistance
Children — over 7yrs welcome
Vegetarian dishes on request
Signposted from Castlebaldwin on the N4, 8 miles north west of Boyle.

GLEBE HOUSE

Collooney, Co Sligo Tel: (071) 67787
Brid and Marc Torrades

In a few short years, Brid and Marc Torrades' Glebe House has become such an integral and enjoyable feature of eating in County Sligo that you can easily overlook the fact that, as a business, this is somewhere which is still a little wet behind the ears.

A tender-yeared operation it may be, and there are improvements to be slowly accomplished with the house as this hard-working couple and their trio of kids balance on their shoestring, but the central thesis of Mrs Torrades's cooking — seasonality, self-sufficiency, clawing in as much local and, indeed, wild food as possible — is a guarantee of food which is drenched with flavour.

She is happy to accept the description of a customer, who just happened to be a French chef, that her style of cooking is 'Cuisine Bourgeois', and further defines her food as 'very simple cooking. Simple and simply decorated, and you cook the food available at the time. Simplicity is the thing'.

There is a well-tempered element of rusticity in her cuisine bourgeois: country terrine with chestnut and cranberry sauce, duck rillettes with an onion confit, venison with bacon and redcurrant, roulade of pork with a light prune sauce. Furthermore, she has the rare gift of being as capable a baker as she is a cook: the vol-au-vent case which cups some wild mushrooms will be as melt-in-the-mouth soft as the puff pastry that enfolds smoked salmon and dill.

Mrs Torrades' affinity with seasonal cooking is very true, and summertime food here dances with fresh flavours, whilst autumn and winter cooking is consoling and comforting. The wine list has a French bias, with some fine country wines from Corbieres — Chateau de Lastours — and the Languedoc — Mas Julien — at very fair prices, wines which suit the autumn and winter menus to perfection. On a busy night service can get rather stretched, but attention to detail with each plate never falters, thus making them worth waiting for.

Open from 6pm Mon-Sun (light lunches in summer from 1pm)
Closed 2 weeks in Jan
Average Price: dinner £16
Credit Cards: Visa, Access/Master, Amex
No Service Charge
Wine Licence
Wheelchair Access (to restaurant, but not toilets)
Children — high chairs, menu £8
Vegetarian option always available
Signposted from Collooney, just before the bridge.

TRUFFLES ★
11 The Mall, Sligo, Co Sligo Tel: (071) 44226
Bernadette O'Shea

Bernadette O'Shea comes from a family of cooks and chefs, a self-critical and very creative family of cooks and chefs, and, when she says — as she has often said — 'I've been thinking a lot about pizzas' — you know she means business.

When Ms O'Shea thinks about pizzas she thinks, first, about the oven: about its heat, its steam, about the tile on which the pizzas sit. She thinks, then about the crust of the pizza, about which combination of flour will give her the result she wants, she thinks about the length of cooking, wonders about how much salt?

She will deliberate on the sauce, wondering what alternative can replace the traditional tomato? She will agonise about what to use to act as a flavour base for fish? She thinks, then, about the toppings: how would caramelised root vegetables fit into the canvas of a pizza base? How can Irish ingredients — anything from farmhouse cheeses to seaweed — be used to expand the language of pizza?

She thinks about the garnishes: the chilli oil, the roasted garlic. She even gets annoyed — quietly, but annoyed all the same — with customers who swap slices of pizza, for so carefully is everything worked out that she will insist that sharing pizzas dilutes the chemistry, the alchemy, the balance, the completeness, which she has worked so hard to achieve.

All this thinking, this agonising, this creativity, goes on endlessly, which means that in the last three years the cooking in Truffles has evolved every bit as quickly as the design of the restaurant has evolved into its current groovy and charming style.

It is this worrying, this thinking, which makes Bernadette O'Shea such a great cook, such an innovator, and it is all this questioning which makes Truffles so successful, so inspired. Like Matisse with his circle of dancers, Ms O'Shea paints, repaints, reiterates and revises her masterpieces, constantly, constantly. The result is an epiphany of culinary pleasure.

Open 5pm-10.30pm Tue-Sun
Closed Xmas
Average Price: dinner £12-£15
No Credit Cards
No Service Charge
Wine Licence
Wheelchair Access (but not to toilets or wine bar)
Children — welcome
Recommended for Vegetarians
The Mall is an extension of Stephen's Street, on the main Enniskillen road, going towards Sligo General Hospital.

CHEZ HANS

Cashel, Co Tipperary Tel: (062) 61177
Hans Peter Matthias

Hans Peter Matthias' superb operation can now confidently celebrate a happy quarter century in business, and it is testament to this man's hard work and acute professionalism that his restaurant — splendidly housed in an old church — feels just as modern as some funky place in Dublin's left bank.

Partly this is because the ambience of Chez Hans is so timeless. It may have been a church at one time, but nowadays this seamless operation buzzes with the motivation and energy of a brasserie. Waiters and waitresses glide and scoot around the tables, ferrying food to famished folk who drive long distances to Cashel to enjoy the unique buzz of the place.

And they come, of course, for the food also, for the cooking is true and accomplished, with a basis of French styling sharpened by a fondness for strong flavours and seasonings and a sturdy grasp of how to utilise Irish ingredients to present them at their best. Portions of whatever you choose — be it fish or shellfish, meat or game, something creamy or something chilly for dessert — are hugely generous, indeed perhaps slightly too much so, but this is likely to be the only cavil you may have about Chez Hans, for the restaurant has evolved its own milieu in the last twenty five years, and that milieu is seductive.

Open 6.30pm-9.30pm Tue-Sat
Closed Xmas, bank holidays and 3 weeks in Jan
Average Price: dinner £22
Credit Cards: Visa, Access/Master
No Service Charge
Restaurant Licence
Wheelchair Access
Children — no facilities
Vegetarian Menu served only on prior arrangement
Just beside the Rock of Cashel, and clearly signposted from the Dublin-Cork road.

DWYER'S OF MARY STREET

5 Mary Street, Waterford, Co Waterford Tel: (051) 77478
Martin Dwyer

Martin Dwyer likes to cook, and it shows. Lettuce and sorrel soup,
monkfish in a herb crust with tapenade, garlic prawns in a rosti
nest, are just some of the signature dishes of a cook who walks that
line between food which maintains his own interest — by virtue
of presenting himself with a constant culinary challenge and by
introducing new foods and new tastes — and yet can manage to make
this food seem comforting and accessible to a somewhat cautious
clientele.

Dwyer has built a rapport with his audience over the last few years,
slowly bringing them along with him as he has matured as a cook,
gradually getting them more involved and eager for more exciting
dishes, whilst always cooking in a style that is considerate and honest.
The restaurant itself is a molly-coddling sort of space, which has
helped his impressive championing of serious food in the town, and
the combination of motherly service, soft music and good food is quite
charming.

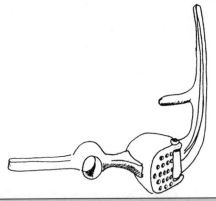

Open 6pm-10pm Mon-Sat
Closed Xmas and bank holidays
Average Price: dinner £18.50 (£12 'early bird')
Credit Cards: Visa, Access/Master, Amex, Diners
No Service Charge
Restaurant Licence
Wheelchair Access
Children — half portions
Vegetarian food served with prior notice
Waterford town centre, near the bridge.

McALPIN'S SUIR INN

Cheek Point, Co Waterford Tel: (051) 82119/82220
Mary and Dunstan McAlpin

On a warmish Wednesday evening in May, maybe on a Thursday in
August when the sun is still bright outside, or perhaps a Friday evening
at anytime of the year, the happy regulars who pack out McAlpin's Suir
Inn sit themselves down on the benches around the walls of this pub,
exhale with pleasure at finding themselves just where they want to be,
and wait for the good, familiar grub which has brought them down to
far-flung Cheekpoint to come wheeling out of the kitchen.
They know what they like, they like what they know, and they know
they will get what they like and what they know everytime. This is one
of the happiest dining places to be found anywhere in the country, and
never mind that it is a boozer. In fact, McAlpin's attracts such devotion
that the behaviour of the customers is reminiscent of the carry on you
get at a religious service. The slightly hushed whispering before the
ritual commences, the automatic calls and responses —
'What would you like?'
'Pint of Guinness, jug of white wine, one fish pie and a prawns in garlic
butter, then two lemon syllabubs'.
'Pie and a prawns here?'.
'Yes, thanks'.
'Syllabubs?'.
'Here, please'.
— then the pealing notes of pleasure as a sense of good grace suffuses
the happy diners. They do good works in McAlpin's, good works
indeed, and you go forth, most definitely, in peace.

Open from 6.30pm Wed-Sat (high season open Tue)
Closed Xmas
Average Price: dinner from £10.50
Credit Cards: Visa, Access/Master
No Service Charge
Full Pub Licence
Wheelchair Access
Children — half portions available
Limited Vegetarian options
Cheek Point is seven miles from Waterford, signpost from the road to Dunmore East.
The restaurant is on the harbour-front.

WATERFORD CASTLE

The Island, Ballinakill, Co Waterford Tel: (051) 78203
Paul McCluskey

Though Waterford Castle is an unapologetic bourgeois stomping ground, don't let this blind you to the fact that Paul McCluskey's food and the invigorating wines you will find here are worthy of anyone's attention, and can be secured at prices which accommodate almost anyone's pocket. Mr McCluskey's cooking is innovative and thoughtful: smoked quail and duck with fennel and baby corn; veal with prunes; salmon rolled in oatmeal on a ginger sauce; lemon sole on a grapefruit butter sauce, excellent vegetarian pastas, all of it intelligent cooking that benefits from impeccable ingredients, and which can be calmly and romantically enjoyed in the rusticated charm of the dining room.

Open 12.30pm-2pm, 7pm-9pm Mon-Sun
Open all year incl Xmas
Average Price: lunch £15.50, dinner £30
Credit Cards: Visa, Access/Master, Amex, Diners
No Service Charge
Full Licence
Wheelchair Access
Children — high chairs
Recommended for Vegetarians
Some three miles outside the town, and well signposted on the Dunmore East road.
Ferry to island runs continually.

CROOKEDWOOD HOUSE

Crookedwood, Mullingar, Co Westmeath Tel: (044) 72165
Noel and Julie Kenny

Noel and Julie Kenny's restaurant occupies a vital role in this quixotic part of the country, where the flatlands of Dublin and Meath quickly expire in the face of a rush of lake water and the topographical ruggedness which signals that you are, suddenly, making your way into the west of the country.

One anticipates dinner in Crookedwood secure in the knowledge that Mr Kenny's skills are capably diverse and that the sensuous combinations he can create will make the hack to Crookedwood worth the bother of all those windy Westmeath roads.

He likes to mix shellfish with pasta — mussels with fettucine, maybe prawns laced with Pernod to accompany the starchy staple — and is a great utiliser of the local venison, served maybe in a gulyas with spatzle, or paired with wild duck in a red wine sauce. Even with the sort of surf 'n' turf specials which ruddy Westmeath appetites savour, Kenny works out the equation by combining a honey-roasted pork steak with salmon in filo and serving it with two sauces.

This is clever cooking, but the intelligence is used to achieve pure, comforting tastes, and the sense of comfort which the Kennys want you to feel runs right through the evening in Crookedwood: service and ambience and comfort make for a baleful experience, a memorable experience.

Open 7.30pm-9.30pm Tue-Sat, 12.30pm-2.30pm Sun
Closed Xmas and bank holidays
Average Price: set dinner £17, Sun lunch £12
Credit Cards: Visa, Access/Master, Amex, Diners
No Service Charge
Full Licence
Wheelchair Access (happy to help)
Children — welcome, half portions
Private room available (seats 40)   Vegetarian options always available
Coming from Mullingar, turn right at the hospital on the road to Castlepollard, then drive to Crookedwood village. Turn right at the Wood pub, then one and a half miles further along you will see the house.

EUGENE'S RESTAURANT ➡ £
Ballyedmond, Co Wexford Tel: (054) 89288
Eugene & Elizabeth Callaghan

Cooking, Curnonsky's famous saying says, is when things taste of themselves. In the unlikely setting of Ballyedmond village — a clatter of thatched cottages, some new bungalows, a couple of shops, kids on bikes and gangly dogs — Eugene Callaghan does his best to top Curnonsky. On occasion, the cooking here seizes flavours which allow things to taste not just of themselves, but also of where they come from. The agreeable climate of the sunny South-East makes for good food. Mr Callaghan adds the final alchemy to transform the good food into great cooking.

His eponymous restaurant sits beside a pub, with a take-away sandwiched in the middle and it is in this trio of establishments that he cooks not just for the restaurant but also for the bar — scrambled eggs with smoked salmon and chives, a selection of seafood with a parsley and garlic butter, panfried steak with mustard cream — and, indeed, for the chipper, where he batters the cod and fries the chips. The dining room of the restaurant itself is a simple, four-square space, pastel-quiet, with the loos immediately at the end of a room which has enough tables to seat thirty or so. The fact that this space leads you to expect little adds to the delight when the food this young man can conjure arrives: roast tomato and bell pepper soup; summer salad with avocado, roast beetroot and cherry tomatoes; breast of chicken stuffed with spinach and bacon; ragout of seafood with a herb cream, all of the dishes infused and suffused with clatteringly delicious tastes.

No other country could offer basic ingredients with these flavours, and one marvels at the ability of this cook to genuflect to the French for direction and inspiration, but to return so confidently to the unique tastes of the Sunny South-East and to be able to extract them and present them on a plate. It's no mean feat to top Curnonsky.

Open 12.30pm-2.30pm Mon-Sun, 7pm-9.30pm Mon-Sun (closed Tues evenings).
Closed Xmas
Average Price: lunch £7.95, dinner from £12
Credit Cards: Visa, Access/Master, Diners
No Service Charge
Full Licence
Wheelchair Access (but not to toilets)
Children — welcome, but no special menu
Vegetarian options always available
Ballyedmond is on the R741 between Gorey and Wexford.

CURTLESTOWN HOUSE COUNTRY RESTAURANT

Enniskerry, Co Wicklow Tel: (01) 282 5083
Colin & Teresa Pielow

In the nicest possible way, Colin and Teresa Pielow's Curtlestown House behaves in that old-fashioned way. You know, somewhere that knows that this year's fancies are passing fancies, someplace that loves the moonlight, loves those old fashioned things: the sound of rain on a window pane, the sorry song that April sings.

Walls in echoingly dark colours and flickering warm fires conspire in a timeless air of grandeur and, together, make you feel good, make you feel welcome, as the ceremony of dinner gets under way. And ceremony is the word: soups are brought in tureens for tables to help themselves and every dish is attractively confected, as well as generous. Elsewhere, the sort of dinner party ambience which Curtlestown engenders might be killingly twee, but here it is just another aspect of a very innocent, old fashioned thing.

A jamboree of flavours runs right through the ceremony of dinner: smoked salmon is good, and so is Caviston's smoked duck with a hazlenut dressing; lamb is fine and sweet, silverside of corned beef has a parsley sauce which is just right, and vegetables are jam-packed with flavour. Puddings are playful nursery productions — chocolate choux buns with banana cream, apple and blackberry crumble — somewhat typical, in fact, of food which is enjoyably restrained and modest, clubbable grub in the old fashioned way, but with none of the depredations of the old Irish way of doing things.

Open 8pm-10pm Tue-Sat, 12.30pm-2.30pm Sun
Open all year, incl Xmas lunch
Average Price: lunch £12, dinner £18
Credit Cards: Visa, Access/Master
No Service Charge
Wine Licence
Limited Wheelchair Access
Children — Sun lunch only, menu £7
Vegetarian meals served on request
Leave Enniskerry on the Glencree Road, up Kilgarron Hill and the restaurant is on the left 2.5 miles along, and brightly lit.

THE OLD RECTORY

Wicklow, Co Wicklow Tel: (0404) 67048 Fax: 69181
Paul & Linda Saunders

The pink painted and tiny Old Rectory is a vital and essential asset to
the town and the County of Wicklow. It is a place which in many ways,
directly reflects the character of Linda Saunders: complex, reserved, pretty
bloody determined, and Mrs Saunders' involved and intricate cooking acts
as a showcase for the strengths and delights of Wicklow itself.

She uses fine organic ingredients, grown locally, which explains firstly
why her food always has a vibrancy and freshness about it, reflecting
the sunshiney, youthful nature of the Wicklow hills.

To this, she brings a degree of invention and expressiveness — and an
intellectual understanding for the architecture of taste — which few
other country house cooks can match. Indeed, the sense of complex
and compatible flavouring in her food is reminiscent of the structure
of a perfume, with alluring scents and mellifluous taste structures to
be enjoyed both in main dishes and in their compatriot sauces: a warm
terrine of salmon and sea trout will swim along with a green herb
sauce, parsnips will pair off with red beans for a soup, whilst the
elegant ruddiness of a carrot and cucumber tart will have the warm
spice of marjoram underpinning it.

Typically, Mrs Saunders takes her skills to the far outreaches of creativity,
constructing dinner menus to arrive at compatible complexity and, to
celebrate the Wicklow Flower Festival, she cooks a daring ten course
Floral Dinner: kale flower purses in filo; gazpacho ropjo with iced borrage
blossoms; roast quail stuffed with apple, pine nut and sage flowers, the
joyful jamboree of tastes is delightfully endless.

The extension of the dining room in this intimate country house has
gifted the Old Rectory with much greater natural light, adding further
to the pleasure of the food, the wines, the experience.

Open 8pm Sun-Thurs, 7.30pm-9pm Fri-Sat
Closed 1 Nov-31 Mar
Average Price: table d'hôte dinner £25
Credit Cards: Visa, Access/Master, Amex, Diners
No Service Charge
Wine Licence
No Wheelchair Access
Children — welcome
Recommended for Vegetarians
30 miles south of Dublin (45 mins), on the left hand side of the road as you enter
Wicklow town, heading South.

THE TREE OF IDLENESS
Sea Front, Bray, Co Wicklow Tel: (01) 286 3498
Susan Courtellas

Few other chef/patrons in Ireland were so intimately associated with
their restaurants as was Akis Courtellas with his much-beloved Tree
Of Idleness. His too-early death robbed the country of a major cooking
talent, for Courtellas had begun in recent years to refine and re-define
the nature of Greek-Cypriot cooking, a cuisine held in low regard for
the most part but which, Courtellas showed, could be raised to heights
of sublime and resonant achievement when in his hands.

Susan Courtellas has continued to run the 'Tree and, assisted by the
devoted staff who ran the show when Akis was alive, she has made the
transition smoothly. The menu is still composed of dishes which Akis
Courtellas either created or upon which he stamped his interpretation
— spinach ravioli filled with chicken mousse and wild mushrooms
with a carrot sauce; grilled ewe's milk cheese with a tahini sauce; three
fillets of beef, lamb and veal in a mustard sauce; smoked lamb with a
blackcurrant and wine sauce.

The great standards of the Eastern Mediterranean — Imam Bayildi,
moussaka, saddle of lamb with feta cheese and olives — are also given
an ever-new interpretation, and the food in the 'Tree can still,
effortlessly, offer flavours that are fresh, exciting and pleasing. The
great dessert trolley, an Archimboldesque explosion of exotic fruits
with accompanying ices and desserts, is unique, the wine list deeply
marvellous and rewarding.

Open 7.30pm-11pm Tue-Sat, 7.30pm-10pm Sun
Closed Xmas and two weeks in early Sept
Average Price: dinner £20
Credit Cards: Visa, Access/Master, Amex, Diners
10% Service Charge
Wine Licence
Wheelchair Access (but 1 step to toilet)
Children — only with advance notice
Vegetarian dishes served each evening
The Tree Of Idleness overlooks the seafront in Bray, and is almost at the end of the
road.

NORTHERN IRELAND
CONTENTS

ANTICA ROMA

67/69 Botanic Ave, Belfast BT7 1JL Tel: (0232) 311121 Fax: 310787
Tony Mura

The success of Antica Roma was always on the cards. Tony Mura's restaurant is part of a small group of Italian eateries in Belfast which cater, with unerring expertise, for different demands, different pockets and different expectations.

In other places which the family own you can get the trattoria stuff with which to fuel a Saturday night or to bring your first teenage date: pizza, pasta, Pavarotti, then some sambucca. But, in Antica Roma Mr Mura has taken a deliberate step upmarket, creating an eating house whose decorations might have been borrowed from the Coliseum but were more likely adapted from a Hollywood sword'n'skirt epic (that's the men in the skirts, by the way: Kirk Douglas, Tony Quinn, perhaps Victor Mature or Richard Burton, with or without Liz).

The lavishness and enormity of the operation allows for it to get packed to the rafters at weekends with serious carousers, and this is when you see AR at its best. The food is a clever revision of standard Italian ideas and you can hit upon an excellent dinner and enjoy some of their splendid Sicilian wines, but the true ethos of the restaurant places high jinks above hâute cuisine.

You are here to enjoy yourself, not to worry about whether they have got their pesto note-perfect or their peppardelle precisely right. The people of Belfast are still not yet prepared to regard Italian food as the gloriously creative and expressive cuisine it truly is, seeing it as more serious than Indian or Chinese cooking, say, but not so serious as French. Antica Roma caters, expertly, for the desire to have food which is familiar yet still a little special, whilst not neglecting the fact that it is the right of every free born man and woman to have one hell of a good time.

Open 6pm-10.45pm Mon-Sat
Closed Xmas, 12 July
Average Price: dinner £17
Credit Cards: Visa, Access/Master, Amex
10% Service Charge
Full Licence
Wheelchair Access (please advise when booking)
Children — welcome
Vegetarian options always available
Half way up Botanic Avenue, just up from Shaftesbury Square.

MANOR HOUSE

47 Donegal Pass, Belfast BT7 Tel: (0232) 238755
Tony Wong

Whilst the Manor House looks just like every other Chinese restaurant — a standard laminate-and-lacquer array of rooms with pling-plong muzak and lurid napery — in a location opposite a thunderously fortified police station which is one the most uninspiring you could possibly imagine, and, whilst you can of course opt for familiar Chinese food if you eat here, Tony Wong's restaurant does take itself more seriously than most, and the real fun only begins when you put them to their mark and bravely put yourself on the culinary edge. The best advice in the Manor House is to order the unusual dishes — fish head, duck's web — and ask for them to be done in the real style, with lots of chillies and authentic seasonings. Their dish of eel with roasted belly of pork, for example, presents these unlikely flavours as perfect bed fellows, the pork sticky and sweet, the eel — from Lough Neagh — sinuous, oily and rich, the glass of Chardonnay in your hand proving to be the perfect complement to a bold and adventurous invention. This sort of adventure allows you to get the best from the Manor House, and to enjoy some of the most authentic and best-realised Chinese food cooked anywhere in the country. Vegetarian menus are excellent, especially with some advance notice.

Open noon-midnight
Closed Xmas
Average Price: lunch from £5.50, dinner £12.50
Credit Cards: Visa, Access/Master, Diners
10% Service Charge
Full Licence
Wheelchair Access
Children — welcome
Full Vegetarian menu available (advance notice required)
Donegal Pass runs off Shaftesbury Square.

NICK'S WAREHOUSE ➡

35/39 Hill Street, Belfast BT1 2LB Tel: (0232) 439690
Nick and Kathy Price

When it comes to the simple business of gifting you with the pleasure, delight and blissful joy of enjoying good food in a restaurant, there are few restaurants in Ireland which can compete with Nick and Kathy Price's Warehouse.

It's not just because the place is comfortable, or that the staff are cool, or that the food is exactly what you want to eat, no matter what time of day you find yourself here: calves' liver with shallots and balsamic vinegar, and a glass of weissbier to drink with this; a lovely vegetarian offering of chestnuts stuffed into cabbage with a tactile and alive tomato sauce or the smart borrowing of that Mosimann speciality of salmon with a vanilla sauce.

This is all vital, of course, but if there is something about Nick's which can truly be said to be its secret, then it is the grace and humour which the Prices give to their work that brings this place alive. The Warehouse, you might say, is a theme restaurant, and the theme is whatever you want it to be. It invites you to Devil-May-Care, at any time of the day or night. If you want to be giddy, then it's giddy. If you want to be smoochy, it's the place to smooch. If you want to enjoy serious food, then you've come to the right place. The winebar downstairs is both intimate and gregarious, the restaurant upstairs is informal and yet just right for dinner-a-deux. Partly this is clever design. Mainly it is the effortlessly achieved atmosphere of the place. Mr Price's eclectic style of cooking — monkfish and crab allied with chilli and soy, an easy-going boudin blanc with a splash of apple sauce, chicken with a plum sauce — is lighthearted and fun and, naturally, Mr Price cracks a joke about it: 'We take our influences from whatever I happen to like at the time. This is the joy of being a restaurateur: you inflict your food on other people'.

Open noon-3pm Mon-Fri, 6pm-9pm Tue-Sat
Closed Xmas Day, Easter, 12th July
Average Price: lunch from £5-£18, dinner £16.95
Credit Cards: Visa, Access/Master, Amex, Diners
No Service Charge (10% on parties of 6 or more)
Full Bar Licence
Wheelchair Access (disabled toilet downstairs for wine bar, lift to restaurant)
Children — in restaurant only
Recommended for Vegetarians
Hill Street is near the old Co-Op building in the centre of Belfast.

ROSCOFF ★ £

7 Lesley House, Shaftesbury Square, Belfast BT2 Tel: (0232) 331532
Paul and Jeanne Rankin

The culinary adventure of Roscoff has been gently chiselled and smoothly refined since the restaurant opened in1989. These days, Paul Rankin's cooking seems devoted not so much to unearthing and evoking tastes as to capturing something approaching the essence of taste. A Herb Risotto with Lobster, for example, will manage to retain the distinct character and individuality of every ingredient: sea-salty shards of shellfish and the earth-ruddy scents of fresh herbs, whilst the clean broth-cooked rice will be soul-satisfying in its quiet simplicity, the whole dish quietly stunning.

The culinary pilgrimage which Roscoff is embarked upon is perhaps best summed up by a remark of Mr Rankin's: 'There's something wonderfully artistic and interesting about pure things', he said. 'It's like a piece of Ardrahan cheese. It is its own simple form of art, and I find it absolutely fascinating'.

This fascination with purity and the search for purity in taste is powered in Mr Rankin by a self-critical awareness which borders on the frenzied. He is obsessively aware of the thin line which separates food that is ordinary from that which is extraordinary, and aware that a kitchen must be endlessly motivated in order to pull off a constant series of culinary coups. Recollections of the food in Roscoff — roasted squab served with shiitake mushrooms, veal meatballs with thin strands of pasta, gloriously simple smoked haddock served with Puy lentils, a crème brûlée as light as breath — summon a style of cooking which takes tremendous risks, and pulls them off.

The ingredients of a modern cosmopolitan style are here, of course, the Cal-Ital and Pacific Rim influences, but the understatement and intuition which Paul Rankin brings to his food is the thing you remember best of all. In this gorgeous eating space, that puritan self-effacement which characterises the North is cast to the wind, and it makes for a thrilling theatre of glamour, glad rags, the good life, Belfast at its very best.

Open 12.30pm-2pm Mon-Fri, 6.30pm-10.30pm Mon-Sat
Closed Xmas, Easter & 12 Jul
Average Price: lunch £14.50, dinner £19.50
Credit Cards: Visa, Access/Master, Amex, Diners
No Service Charge
Full Licence
Full Wheelchair Access
Children — welcome, menu from £7
Recommended for Vegetarians
On Belfast's 'Golden Mile' leading from the city centre to the university.

RAMORE

The Harbour, Portrush, Co Antrim Tel: (0265) 824313
George McAlpin

The re-invention of the Ramore into a more informal dining space, with the kitchen fully open to view and a set of bar chairs at the counter, has lightened the atmosphere of this swishest of dining rooms, set high up in the harbour at Portrush.

The paraphernalia of a working kitchen — the brigade of whisks, the tumbling tresses of garlic, the bottles of oil, the dog-eared texts, are all on happy exhibition along with their white-clad employers, who intersect with one another with the sure-footedness of dancers. It's a charming entertainment, as you sip aperitifs and nibble bread, but when the food arrives, it is quickly, strictly, heads-down.

In parallel with the renovation, George McAlpin's cooking has shifted its concentration away from an obsessively detailed French style, bringing on board more of the lighter influences of the Pacific Rim: Japan, San Francisco, Thailand, Indonesia, with considered borrowings from the Mediterranean.

This lighter style is delivered with confident aplomb: a quintet of tempura prawns fanned around a big white plate, their crisp, ochre batter offset by the bright playfulness of finely diced peppers tucked under a trio of Mexican tostados, a quiet dish of tagliatelle with a slurpy Roquefort sauce and shards of bacon. Then, some monkfish with utterly splendid local scallops, lightly coated in breadcrumbs and their saline succulence perfectly captured by quick frying, and some char-grilled chicken with the sharpness of red onions and the sweetness of sun-dried tomatoes for annotation. Seasonal vegetables are crisp, a garlicky purée of spuds delicious, desserts of serene lemon tart and a cracking praline ice-cream perfectly delivered. The staff are super, the wine list short and clever, breads are excellent, prices are keen and the whole organisation devoted to delivering the sort of good time it is otherwise almost impossible to find nowadays in fripperish Portrush.

Open 7pm-10pm Tue-Sat (wine bar downstairs open for lunch)
Closed Xmas and 2 weeks in Mar
Average Price: dinner £25
Credit Cards: Visa, Access/Master
No Service Charge
Restaurant Licence
Wheelchair Access to restaurant, but not to toilets
Children — controlled children welcome
Vegetarian options available with notice
On the harbour in Portrush.

ADELBODEN COUNTRY HOUSE INN

Donaghadee Road, Groomsport BT19 2LG, Co Down Tel: (0247) 464288
Fax: 270053
Denis and Margaret Waterworth

Dennis Waterworth saw a description of his wife in these celebrated words of Henry Ford, a description so fitting and appropriate, indeed, that he had a plaque made for the restaurant, bearing the famous quotation:
'You can do anything if you have enthusiasm. Enthusiasm is the yeast that makes your hopes rise to the stars, is the sparkle in your eyes, the swing in your gait, the grip of your hand, the irresistible surge of will and energy to execute your ideas. Enthusiasts are fighters. They have fortitude. They have staying quality. Enthusiasm is at the bottom of all progress. With it there is accomplishment. Without it there are only alibis.'
There are no alibis in the Adelboden, but there is yeast in their stratospheric efforts, and will and energy, and fortitude. The Adelboden is a wonderfully motivated restaurant, though the quiet nature of the place and the conservative cooking could escape you if you want stylishness at the expense of strength of character, or affectation instead of authenticity. The Waterworths and their charming, devoted staff keep it bubbling along — enthusiastically! — for twelve hours a day, offering first a lunch menu, then afternoon tea, then high tea and finally dinner.
Their aim is to cook food which you want to eat and which will give you delight: no showy bravado from the kitchen, just the simple business of service. Vegetarians get their own full menu: cauliflower beignet with a green peppercorn hollandaise sauce; vegetable stroganoff with basmati rice; wholewheat crêpes, and there are even veggie choices for kids. The plain eaters of North Down can have steak, a real beef burger or battered cod with home-made chips. Culinary dare-devils can choose their own sauces for fish or pasta. At all times, to all tastes, the verity of Margaret Waterworth's cooking is immensely pleasing.

Open noon-10pm Tue-Sat
Closed 25th-26th Dec (open on bank holiday Mondays)
Average Price: lunch £3.75-£9.50, dinner £15
Credit Cards: Visa, Access/Master
No Service Charge
Restaurant Licence
Full Wheelchair Access
Children — special menu £3.25
Full Vegetarian Menu
Clearly signposted on the coast road to Donaghadee, just outside Groomsport.

BACK STREET CAFÉ

The Vennel, 14 Queen's Parade, Bangor, Co Down Tel: (0247) 453990
Peter Barfoot

'The exterior has the feel of the entrance to an air raid shelter', was
how a friend described the appearance of the Back Street Café, whilst
another remembered the lane down which you walk to find the Café
as a place where you scampered for 'Kissin', pissin' and fightin''.
Pay no attention to the grotty lane or the grim exterior. Inside, the Café
is a swarth of warm ochre colours on rough plastered walls, the kitchen
is open-plan, the waiting staff cool and laid-back in their work, and Mr
Barfoot's cooking is the final trump in this unlikely place.
The daily menu does not neglect the conventional preferences of the
North Down diner — pork fillet, chargrilled sirloin steak, saddle of
lamb — but whilst the lamb will have a conventional port and
redcurrant sauce, the steak teams up with an unusual beurre de cepe
and the lamb enjoys a rich Madeira demi-glace. This is the cleverness
of the Café: this food will not frighten anyone at first glance, but there
are so many enjoyable twists, turns and revisions at work that the
conventional is transmuted, and transformed. Mr Barfoot likes to pair
turbot with a smoked garlic beurre blanc, will tilt some Calvados and
roast baby pears to cut the warm cream sauce of roast pork, uses
chives to freshen the beurre blanc served with tiny queen scallops, or
perhaps some sun-dried tomatoes for the little shellfish.
The modern stylishness extends through to desserts: rich autumn
pudding, smooth vanilla terrine, bramble ice-cream with cassis coulis.
The occasional concoction will be wonderfully wrong-headed, it must
be said, and vegetarians do not do well here: the Café needs to take
their requests more seriously and to create something, rather than
offering a mere grab-bag of meat-free stuff.
At weekends, everyone brings along their own bottles of plonk and settles
into an atmosphere that is stratospheric with the relentless Northern
zeitgeist: eat, drink, be merry, and let tomorrow take care of itself.

Open 7.30pm-10pm Tue-Sat
Closed Xmas
Average Price: dinner under £20
Credit Cards: Visa, Access/Master
No Service Charge
No Licence (bring your own)
Wheelchair Access to restaurant, but not to toilets
Children — no facilities
Vegetarian food cooked to order
The Vennel is a laneway leading off Queen's Parade opposite the seafront in Bangor.

DEANE'S ON THE SQUARE
Station Square, Co Down Tel: (0247) 852841/273155
Haydn & Michael Deane

There are modern and modish influences visibly at work in Deane's On The Square. The semi-revealed kitchen, tantalising with its glimpses of speedy work-in-progress by white-clad cooks, evokes, firstly, a bistro ambience, whilst the creative sounds of sizzle-sizzle that extrude from it quickly puncture the cloistered atmosphere of this enlivened old station building, as do the picturesque but vaguely vague waiters with their maneish pony-tails.

The copy of Ian McAndrew's 'Fish Cookery' sat on a window ledge signals the direction of Michael Deane's cookery. He is fond of the pyrotechnics of preparation and elaboration, and then the robust use of colour on a plate, as crisp orange carrots intersect with bushy green broccoli interleaved around pillows of salmon with baby scallops, or coins of lamb sit astride a splendidly clever turban of potato purée, finished off with a crisp grated potato cake.

These are clever moves away from the suburban signatures which other aspects of Deane's curtsey to for the benefit of their clientele: dull music, an obvious wine list, a crowded little bar downstairs, severely-trimmed prices. But the confidence that will come with extra experience should see Deane's relax a little more, especially as their opening period in business has proven to be such a success that they have already had to extend the premises. This should allow Deane's to see the full benefits of Michael Deane's cooking, for this is a talented chef and there are good tastes here — a fine duck terrine set off with carefully placed summer salad leaves and an appropriate walnut dressing, a reverberant shellfish sauce around a seafood sausage, softly poached pears with a bitingly intense blackcurrant sorbet — and the nocturnal boredom of Helen's Bay will be happily shattered by the frivolous delight of happy customers.

Open 7pm-10pm Tue-Sat, 12.30pm-2.30pm Sun
Closed Xmas
Average Price: lunch £11.50, dinner from £15
Credit Cards: Visa, Access/Master, Amex
No Service Charge
Restaurant Licence
No Wheelchair Access
Children — welcome high chairs
Vegetarian options always available
The restaurant overlooks the station platform in Helen's Bay. Look for the newly-restored tower.

IONA BISTRO

27 Church Road, Holywood, Co Down Tel: (0232) 425655
Bartjan Brave

The Iona Bistro is — almost — a fail-safe. You bring along your own
bottles of wine, sit on the steep stairs quaffing your plonk as you wait
for a table, and then enjoy not only the breezy familiarity of a true
bistro — gingham tablecloths, candles stuffed into wine bottles, hassled
waiters, the roar of conversation, the steady backbeat of well-chosen
music, the expectation that you are certain to know someone at an
adjoining table — but also food that is packed with true tastes.
The blackboarded menus offer a trio of starters and main dishes, with an
unannounced vegetarian choice always available, and then probably a
quartet of desserts, and no matter what you choose, Bartjan Brave's food is
always distinguished by simplicity, voluble, lively tastes, and good value.
An excellent grained mustard dressing picks up a straightforward salad
of avocado and melon, a cauliflower and cheese soup is rich and
warming, the peanut sauce on a lamb kebab well-realised. Salmon
will be lightly grilled and served with a serene cucumber sauce, lamb
adorned with gracious tastes of rosemary, a vegetarian stir-fry shaken
up with a good cashew nut sauce.
With simple fried potatoes and crisp salad leaves, this is relaxed,
welcoming food. Familiar, of course, but the comfort of these true tastes
means that you could eat this food most every night and not tire of it.

Open 10am-4.30pm 6.30pm-midnight Mon-Sat
Closed Xmas
Average Price: lunch £5, dinner £12
No Credit Cards
No Service Charge
No Licence (bring your own)
No Wheelchair Access
Children — no facilities
Recommended for Vegetarians
Holywood town centre, up the stairs over the Iona Wholefood Shop.

SULLIVAN'S

Sullivan Place, Holywood, Co Down Tel: (0232) 421000
Simon Shaw

If Hollywood, U.S.A., has the stars, the movie lots and the sort of restaurants where you can expect to spy Richard Gere and Julia Roberts, then Holywood, County Down, may not have the stars or the movie lots, but it does have the restaurants. One must admit, perhaps sadly, that it does not have those restaurants where you can expect to spy Richard Gere and Julia Roberts but, then, who can have everything? If you want Richard and Julia, get a video.

Sullivan's is Simon Shaw's first venture out on his own, after long tenures under Paul Rankin in Roscoff, just up the road in Belfast, as well as spells working in France and Switzerland and then a period when he carved interesting and enjoyable menus in Santé, just down the road. The restaurant's almost-instantaneous success has presented this amorphous village with a happy increase to its already considerable culinary riches.

Sullivan's works as a coffee shop by day and transmutes into a restaurant in the evening when the glasses and the napery come out. Mr Shaw's menus show the imprint of a solid, reassuring cook: Loin of Pork with Sweet and Sour Red Cabbage; Braised Duck Leg with Polenta Mash; Salmon and Courgettes with a Vanilla Cream Sauce. If the food is modern in influence, then tastes can seem age-old and pleasingly sedate, especially with soups and staples.

Prices are very keen and the fact that you can bring your own wine allows for the cost of a cab fare to wherever you hail from. Something, it must be said, should be done about the music   Mr Shaw should borrow a leaf from his old stomping ground of Roscoff and search out sounds that are suitable and soothing, and not the rather silly stuff one hears at present.

Open 10am-4pm Mon-Sat, 6pm-10pm Tue-Sat
Closed Xmas and bank holidays
Average Price: lunch £3.95, dinner £14.95
Credit Cards: Visa, Access/Master, Diners
10% Service Charge for parties of 6 or more
No Licence (bring your own)
No Wheelchair Access
Children — half portions
Vegetarian meals always available
Holywood town centre.

BEECH HILL COUNTRY HOUSE HOTEL ➡
32 Ardmore Road, Derry, Co Londonderry Tel: (0504) 49279 Fax: 45366
Seamus Donnelly

The menu in the Beech Hill is one of those intriguingly quiet
productions, not much more than titles with some elaboration typed
in plain print underneath: Fresh Irish Salmon — resting on a potato
galette and surrounded by a rich pesto sauce. Fillet of Turbot — with a
thyme scented sauce and accompanied by a wild rice and fish mousse
timbale. Confit of Duck — upon a bed of pickled red cabbage and
served with a green peppercorn sauce.
It sounds clever, of course, not too ambitious and full of suggestions
which suggest deliciousness — red cabbage and duck partner perfectly,
pesto and salmon go hand in glove. The food here is the work of a shy,
quiet young man, Noel McMeel, and his ability to stride that danger zone
wherein a cook must satisfy the conservative nature of his customers and,
at the same time, create food which inspires his own imagination, is one
of the most delicious resolutions in the world of Irish food.
With things that are timeworn and, it seems, uninspiring, McMeel
achieves a fusion of tastes and a synthesis of food cultures that has
delight jumping out of every dish: avocado mousse on a cucumber
spaghetti; a filo parcel of mushrooms on a bed of lentils with a mild
curry sauce; a seafood sausage sitting on softly stewed baby leeks with
a prawn sauce all around; Dublin Bay Prawns with a julienne of
courgettes and homemade ravioli
However he does manage it, his ability to combine tried and trusted
favourite tastes with forays into modern styling and technique is nothing
but a joy, and with increased experience McMeel has begun to transcend
the lessons learnt at the hands of other fine chefs — a love of colourful
complexity borrowed from Ian McAndrew, a love of earthy flavours
brought from Paul Rankin — and has begun to sign dishes with his own
signature. You don't expect food of this order in an hotel, and to find it
in the quiet, shy dining room in Beech Hill is purest pleasure.

Open noon-2.30pm, 6pm-9.45pm Mon-Sun
Closed 24-25 Dec
Average Price: lunch from £11.50, dinner from £17.95
Credit Cards: Visa, Access/Master, Amex
No Service Charge
Full Licence
Wheelchair Access (but 1 step to toilet)
Children — high chairs and half portions
Recommended for Vegetarians
Beech Hill is signposted from the A2, just past Drumahoe as you come into Derry on
the main Belfast road.

Brandy:
The Essence of the Essence

CHAMPAGNE IS FOR parties, wine is for dinner, pints are for pubs, whiskey is for friends, but brandy, amongst all the drinks of the world, performs perhaps the most sociable double act of any tipple.

Brandy is for soloists, and for sharing. 'The essence of the essence of the grape', as it has been described, is the most private and singular of drinks, with a claustral character that means it can be enjoyed by an individual, all alone. Yet it is also a most gregarious and social alcohol, adding an atmosphere to a post-dinner reverie which suggests intimacy, true friendship.

Where port tends to be boisterous, brandy is subtle; not just the perfect digestif but also a drink which, at ten in the morning, can be enjoyed with gusto, for it will leave you with a clear head, even after a couple of glasses.

A few more than a few glasses, however, and you may find yourself blithely echoing the words of that stertorous old bore, Dr Johnson, who — and one has to believe that it was after a skinful of Cognac — declared that: 'Claret is the liquor for boys; port for men; but he who aspires to be a hero must drink brandy'.

Brandies are distilled all over the world, but those with the greatest histories and reputations are, of course, made in France, and specifically in Cognac and Armagnac. Rather than simply being referred to under the generic name 'brandy', a development of the original Dutch name for the drink, 'brandewijn', which translates literally as 'burnt wine', Cognac and Armagnac trumpet their superior status by calling their distilled drinks after their regions.

In fact, both areas — Cognac is north of Bordeaux on the west coast of France, Armagnac little more than a hundred miles south and further inland — then distinguish further and delineate the spirits by reference to those areas surrounding the towns in which the grapes are grown.

In Cognac, spirit produced in a concentric area of chalky land around the town itself and south of the River Charente is called Grand Champagne, the immediate concentric land is Petite Champagne, with a small patch north known as Borderies. These areas, thanks to land so chalky it is comparable to Champagne in northern France, produce the most refined cognac. Surrounding them are three further areas, the Bois. The predominant grape planted is Ugni Blanc, which is bad for wine-making but perfect for distilling.

In Armagnac, the best brandies come from the plain known as Bas-Armagnac, with the area known as Ténarèze to the east, around the town of Condom, the next in ranking, and the surrounding Haut-Armagnac the largest area.

'Armagnac shares only its subtlety and its very high standards with cognac, for the two brandies are poles apart in style and in the techniques used to make them', writes Hugh Johnson, and one need not even so much as open a bottle to prove his assertion. Armagnac is dark, suggestive of nuts and hot sun, suggestive of the South, whilst Cognac impresses with its paleness and austerity, its restraint. It is Cognac, it seems, which strives to be 'the essence of the essence': Armagnac is content to be less ethereal, to offer more pungency, a whippier embrace of alcohol.

In practical terms, distillation methods differ between the two regions, and whilst Cognac is dominated by those famous brand names we all know — Hennessy (hailing originally from Ireland, of course), Martell, Rémy Martin and Courvoisier — Armagnac is a place of smallish producers.

The world-known merchants have not made their reputations merely by marketing, however. The Cognacs made by the 'big four' all have a recognisable individuality: Courvoisier's style of cognac is 'unmistakable, richer, smoother, more caramelly than any other' writes Nicholas Faith in his 'Guide to Cognac and other Brandies'. The Hennessy style is 'round, full and fruity', Martell cognacs have 'a certain nuttiness . . . though recently some of the brandies seem to have become rather richer to suit the oriental palate', whilst Rémy Martin's signature is 'undeniably smooth and attractive, with some depth and fruit'.

If there is a rule with the brandies of the big four, it is to select their most choice bottles. With Courvoisier, for example, the standard 3 Star Luxe is warm and honeyed in the mouth but has a certain torchiness. The VSOP (Very Special Old Pale — the names and stars given by brandy makers to their wares have relatively little meaning) is more balanced and has a greater architecture of tastes, whilst the Napoleon is in another class altogether: smoothly sweetish with those typical characteristics we hope from Cognac — subtlety, perseverance of flavour and a long after-taste. You pay perhaps three times as much for the Napoleon as the 3 Star Luxe, but the extra money is well spent.

It is when we enter the realm of the specialist wine merchants, however, that we begin to track down those brandies whose individuality portends the work of an individual. Chateau de Beaulon, for example, is a cognac produced by organic methods with the grapes coming from a single vineyard. Christian Thomas also uses two extra grape types to blend with the ubiquitous Ugni Blanc: Folle Blanche and Colombard. In the VSOP this gives a brandy with a remarkably light and effervescent character that dances with flavour. M. Thomas also makes a famous Pineau des Charentes, a mixture of grape juice and cognac, which is fulsome with vanilla and elderflower flavours.

A similar singularity is found in the cognacs made by the Lhéraud family, perhaps because once again a small proportion of Folle Blanche and Colombard grapes is used, and grown by natural methods in a single vineyard. Here, in their Réserve du Templier, the brandy is broader and sits with a honeyed disposition on the tongue before a slight suggestion of pruneiness begins to thread its way out from the after-taste. It is the balance of the Lhéraud cognacs which impresses, along with their warmth and the wrap of suggestive aromas. Their bottle, clouded with green wax and simple as a wimple, is also a delight.

It is the delivery of a solid aftertaste which impresses with the Payrault cognacs made by the Vallet family, best known for their Château Montifaud brandies. There is a time delay as this especially dark and rich textured drink slips away, but then kapow! and the head fills with aromatic scents of honey and plant-nectar.

Where the Payrault taste is dark and broad, that of Prunier is smooth and clean, never more so than with their 20 Years Old cognac. Initially, one imagines that the scents and aromas of the brandy have receded, this drink is so slender, but then the architecture of the cognac's flavours fill the mouth and the essences seem to float up into the top of your head. The alcohol seems encased in an overcoat of warmth which reverberates around the mouth, creating a deliciously delicate drink.

For sheer distinctiveness, however, probably nothing matches Delamain's Pale and Dry. Sherry-gold in colour, light as a Philip Treacy hat, the Pale and Dry is an intense encounter with the ethereal that leaves you chafing for more as the brandy slips away. The interplay of flavours is as complex as a game of chess and everything is so sublimated and understated that it is impossible to put your finger on just what gives the brandy its character, other than its evanescence.

Indeed it is this meeting of the mellifluous that gives good cognac its teasing, tremulous sense of delight, its intoxicating element. Most alcohol aims to bowl you over, but cognac pulls the rug from under your feet, waits to surprise you with its essences and flavours, prefers subtlety to any manner of strong-arm.

The cognacs of Pierre Ferrand are fine examples of the typicity which you should seek when buying cognac, the traces of vanilla and orange, the suggestion of prune and wood, the construct of scents and aromas forming a slowly-evolving panorama of flavours in the mouth.

Armagnac, by contrast, seems aristocratic but more sensual, its colour deeper, its nature seemingly more virile. As Nicholas Faith writes of the armagnacs of Marquis de Caussade, 'the brand itself is light, but full and aromatic', helped by the fact that Caussade armagnacs are often of very considerable age — their VSOP is at least ten years old, rather than the necessary 4 years.

Those brandies that hail from the region known as Bas-Armagnac seem best to evoke the scents of nuts and fruits, with something of the sugary clout of a Christmas cake. In the Samalens VSOP one finds a trace of what is known as rancio, a term for the richness which a brandy can develop after twenty or so years in cask: odours of sultana and prune, caramel and burnt toast, but the structure of the brandy houses these robust elements perfectly, making this a lush, strapping armagnac.

By contrast, the bas armagnacs of Château de Laubade are more controlled, with elements of honey and citrus peel floating around at the canvas and a very pleasing directness of taste.

In between these two, the armagnacs of Château du Tariquet have a richly voluble smartness of flavour which suggests honeycomb as you sip it, then suggests apple scents and, then, simply suggests that you have another glass.

For this is the beauty of cognac and armagnac. They are subtle and seductive, their bottles as slender as sin and as moral as the next morning. Cautionary yet castaway, private yet personable, they entice, and you succumb.

Index

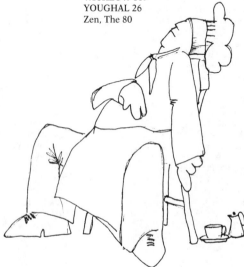

OTHER TITLES FROM ESTRAGON PRESS

The Bridgestone Irish Food Guide

André Simon Special Award-winning Bridgestone Irish Food Guide is the most comprehensive, independent, critical guide to the very best food in Ireland. From the most committed and creative artisan food producers north and south to the finest restaurants east and west, the Bridgestone Irish Food Guide explores and describes in extensive detail Ireland's inspiring, blossoming food culture. Price: £11.99

The Bridgestone 100 Best Places to Stay in Ireland

From simple B&Bs to grand Country Houses, from welcoming Farmhouses to luxurious Hotels, this book finds the best places to stay in Ireland. Price: £5.99

The Bridgestone 100 Best Places to Eat in Dublin

The definitive critical independent guide to the finest meals in Dublin, from pizzerias to the grandest restaurants. Simply the essential guide to the capital city's best food. Price: £5.99

The Bridgestone Vegetarian's Guide to Ireland

A comprehensive guide for vegetarians to the finest Irish vegetarian food, written in the style of the award-winning Bridgestone Irish Food Guide. Covering every possible food source, from farms and shops through to restaurants and the best accommodation, this is the definitive guide for vegetarians. Price: £6.99

All titles in the Bridgestone Series from Estragon Press are available in good book stores nationwide.

If you missed any of the Series or have trouble getting them locally, they can be ordered by post direct from the publisher.

Simply fill out the coupon below, enclosing a cheque or money order for the correct amount (add £1.50 per book for postage and packing), and the relevant title(s) will be dispatched to you immediately. Be sure to fill out your address completely, and to print carefully.

Please send me the following title(s) from the Bridgestone series (please tick):

☐ **The Bridgestone Irish Food Guide £11.99**

☐ **The Bridgestone Vegetarian's Guide to Ireland £6.99**

☐ **The Bridgestone 100 Best Places to Eat in Dublin £5.99**

☐ **The Bridgestone 100 Best Restaurants in Ireland £5.99**

☐ **The Bridgestone 100 Best Places to Stay in Ireland £5.99**

I enclose a cheque/money order (delete) for £_____ (including P&P)

....

Name..

Address ....

....

....

....

SEND TO: Estragon Press, Durrus, Co Cork, Ireland